Sarah Baker

The Jewish Twins

Sarah Baker

The Jewish Twins

ISBN/EAN: 9783743310643

Manufactured in Europe, USA, Canada, Australia, Japa

Cover: Foto ©ninafisch / pixelio.de

Manufactured and distributed by brebook publishing software (www.brebook.com)

Sarah Baker

The Jewish Twins

THE JEWISH TWINS.

BY

AUNT FRIENDLY.

"Pray for the peace of Jerusalem: they shall prosper that love thee."

NEW YORK:
ROBERT CARTER & BROTHERS,
No. 530 BROADWAY.
1861.

Entered according to Act of Congress, in the year 1860, by

ROBERT CARTER & BROTHERS,

In the Clerk's Office of the District Court for the Southern District of New York.

CONTENTS.

CHAP.		PAGE
I.	—A PRESENT	5
II.	—NAOMI'S BOYS	11
III.	—THE LITTLE FRIEND	16
IV.	—PERCUSSION CAPS	26
V.	—HUPPIM'S VISIT	34
VI.	—THE DREADED NAME	43
VII.	—THE PLAY-FELLOWS' MEETING	48
VIII.	—PURIM AT JACOB MYERS'	55
IX.	—THE OLD GENTLEMAN	64
X.	—THE REWARD CARD	76
XI.	—THE PASSOVER	85
XII.	—BEGINNINGS	97
XIII.	—THE SICK-ROOM	109
XIV.	—GOOD NEWS	118
XV.	—A YOUNG DISCIPLE	128
XVI.	—BRAVO	135
XVII.	—THE ANNOUNCEMENT	143
XVIII.	—THE PRISONER	152
XIX.	—DISCIPLINE	159
XX.	—MUPPIM	164
XXI.	—A RESOLUTION	177
XXII.	—A SURPRISE	186
XXIII.	—THE OUTWARD SIGN	194
XXIV.	—THE TRUE PASSOVER	197
XXV.	—A REMOVAL	200
XXVI.	—A CHRISTIAN FAMILY	203
XXVII	—CONCLUSION	206

THE JEWISH TWINS.

I.

A Present.

JACOB MYERS had a little shop on a well-known street-corner, in one of our Atlantic cities.

There, on pleasant days, ladies came to buy cheap edgings, and even in rainy weather there were customers who stopped for a paper of pins, or for a spool of "40 cotton," while Jacob's wife sat sewing behind the counter.

Jacob was not much in the shop, himself; he spent his time in making trips into the country, to sell a part of his stock at the stray farm-houses, and in the wayside villages. Jacob had learned to go to the back door when he was refused at the front, and he was sure to lighten his pack and make more heavy his purse, at every kitchen he entered. He had gilt jewelry to suit all tastes, and combs for "a mere song," not to speak of laces and buttons, at what he declared to be "next to nothing" prices.

Jacob was not out with his pack at the time when our story begins. No! He was in his own shop, looking the very picture of happiness. Jacob had just received a present, worth exactly twice as much as the thing he had long most wished for.

Now you must not be thinking of purses of gold, or cargoes of lace edgings. Jacob valued such things enough, and too much doubtless, but he valued still more the gifts a kind hand had sent him.

Back of the shop was the small "family room," with a stair-case leading out of it into the chamber above.

In that upper room were Jacob's treasure's—two little black-eyed baby-boys, twins, as "alike as two peas," and each looking about him, as if much astonished at finding himself in such a queer world, with such a queer little brother at his side.

Jacob's wife, Naomi, seemed as well pleased as her husband, and there was a sweet, placid joy in her face as she lay there, with her twin-babies beside her.

For some unknown reason, people choose to give twins names just as nearly alike as possible, without being exactly the same, as if it were not puzzling enough to have two tiny things tottering about, the very pictures of each other, without adding to the difficulty.

Jacob Myers, however, was not wiser than the rest of mankind in this particular, as we shall soon see.

Jacob had a book which contained the

names which pleased him best, yet even there he was puzzled to suit himself for the twins. Jacob's book was a Hebrew copy of the Old Testament; of the New Testament he, poor man! knew nothing.

Jacob was a Jew, one of the same nation who once occupied the land of Canaan, who were there in the time of our Saviour, and are now scattered over the wide earth.

Wherever the Jew goes, he takes with him his Holy Book, the Old Testament. Even poor Jews can often read Hebrew, and we have lately heard of a travelling pedler's surprising some theological students, at their Hebrew studies, by reading to them, freely, from the Old Testament, in the language in which it was written.

Jacob read the Scriptures as a duty, though we cannot say that it was with devoutness, or prayer.

Now, up and down the genealogies Jacob searched and searched, but at last his eye brightened—he had happened upon just the thing for his purpose. There were the names of the sons of Benjamin—"Muppim" and "Huppim"! Why, Jacob verily thought Benjamin must have been blessed like himself, with two babies at once! The names were certainly meant for twins! The discovery was forthwith announced to Naomi, who consented to the choice without a word of objection; she did not feel like entering into a discussion then, for various reasons. Those two black-eyed boys had a preciousness to her that could be expressed by no name; no words could tell it, but it throbbed deep down in her true mother's heart.

Naomi had been speaking to some one in her quiet room, when she had been alone with her babies. Of course she had talked to them in her own soft, cooing, loving way; made dear little sounds that even a baby ought to understand—but that is not what we mean. Naomi had spoken, slowly, solemnly, and distinctly, words of thanksgiving to the God of Israel for the great blessing He had bestowed upon her. She had asked the peculiar care of the Lord for her little ones, and given them back to Him who had just given them to her. She would bring them up in the fear of the Lord, and in the fulfilment of His Law.

With these pious thoughts in her mind, Naomi fell asleep, to dream of seeing wings sprouting from the fat shoulders of her baby-boys, and the little things themselves soaring away to Heaven, as if already too good for earth.

II.

Naomi's Boys.

JACOB soon tired of his quiet home-life, though he had many a chance to refresh himself by playing with his babies, for he was not troubled with a constant run of customers.

He was quite glad when Naomi was once more sitting in the shop with her needle in her hand. She had double use for it now that the twins had come.

There they lay, (Muppim and Huppim they had duly been named,) and in the great basket by their mother they nestled, two warm, funny little things, the wonder of all the neighborhood.

Naomi's shop suddenly grew popular. The children would not buy their slate-pencils anywhere else. Lonely apprentice girls stopped there to get needles and have a peep at the babies, and the ladies seemed to want more edgings than ever before. One rich, childless widow fairly frightened Naomi by the covetuous way in which she looked at the little dears. She even went so far as to ask Naomi whether she could not part with one of them.

Naomi would have had her own black eyes put out with a hot iron sooner. So she told the lady plainly; and then the stranger looked so displeased, and went out so quickly, that Naomi began to fear that harm was coming to her babies, and that it was hardly safe to let two such treasures be seen by every chance customer. Babies had been stolen—she had heard of such a thing! She was half-sorry she had let Jacob go off, with his full pack on his back, a week ago. He came home that night, and had a hearty laugh at Naomi about her fears. That laugh did her real good, and was worth more than a whole half hour of reasoning. The way that Jacob snugged up the little creatures under his great coat, showed how dear they were to him, and yet he did not seem afraid of losing them! Not he!

He said this was a free country, and even a poor Jew need not be afraid of harm's coming to his humble home.

What a blessing it is to live in a country that is a safe refuge for the ancient people of God! So Naomi thought, and a kindly spirit rose in her towards her adopted home, and from that day it was dearer to her than the forsaken Poland of her childhood.

Yes, Muppim and Huppim got on to their two feet, or rather their four feet, if we speak of them together, and tottered about the shop, without once suspecting that anybody could despise a Jew.

The world seemed a very pleasant place to the little fellows, for Naomi had taught them to obey while they were in her arms, and, now that they could run alone, they felt the advantage of being wisely ruled. Muppim and Huppim had others than their mother to cast sunshine on their daily life.

The droll ways of the two round-headed little brothers made friends of their mother's customers, and Naomi's face was often brightened by the kind words bestowed on her children.

Years went by, and the twins, like other boys, passed from frocks to jackets and trowsers, and from thinking their mother the wisest woman in the world, to quite too good an opinion of themselves.

You must not think that the brothers resembled each other as closely all this time as they did when they first lay in the basket together.

Before many months had passed over their heads, Muppim gave signs of a "great sensible nose," and Huppim's mouth began to fill up with big teeth, that quite changed his expression. As their characters grew more decided the differences increased, and Muppim's thoughtful look was as unlike Huppim's merry glance, as were his quiet, sage sayings to the droll speeches of his brother.

Strangers still continued to take one for the other, and the boys often had their own fun with the customers in this way; but persons who knew them well had no trouble in distinguishing them at once. Naomi's joy in her children increased every year; and when they were eight years old she was heard to say, that the little fellows were the best boys, to her belief, in the whole city.

III.

The Little Friend.

JACOB and Naomi Myers had lived for several years in the same house before their children were born, yet they had not made a single acquaintance among their neighbors. They had a few Jewish friends in other parts of the city, but Naomi was not fond of visiting. She was shy and home-loving by nature, and Jacob was away so much of his time that he was glad to spend his Sabbaths with his wife, and cared little for other company.

It is not to be supposed that Muppim and Huppim would settle down to such a secluded life. As soon as they were able to play on the pavement they made acquaintances among the boys of the neighborhood, and ere long had a special favorite among them. Muppim and Huppim had not all their time for play now; they had work to do, and tasks to learn, and they were beginning, too, to be of assistance to their mother in the shop. It was a proud day to Muppim when he sold his first paper of pins, and Huppim soon was able to boast of having correctly made change for a dime in the sale of a skein of sewing-silk!

Naomi was not hard upon her twins; she knew that when other children were out with their sleds, her boys, too, wanted to share the fun. When Charlie Fay put in his curly head, to ask if Muppim and Huppim might come out to play with him, Naomi rarely said "No!"

Naomi liked Charlie Fay, partly because her children liked his fair, sunny face, and partly because he had a gentle look in his blue eyes, and such tones in his voice as are heard where there is a kindly, well-governed character.

Often, while the boys were at play, Naomi's glance followed them through the glass door of the shop, and that glance was full of love to them. Naomi's love found a way of winning blessings for her children. Not only did she pray for them morning and evening, but through the long day there was prayer in her heart for them. She was ever asking the mercy of the God of Israel for them, and pleading that they might be guided into the knowledge of His will.

The Old Testament, in Hebrew, was Naomi's delight; she loved to hear Jacob read it on Sabbath evenings, and many of its beautiful passages she had treasured in her memory. She might be heard repeating the Psalms of David to herself, as she sat at her work, or saying aloud some of the sublime passages in Isaiah.

Naomi was a Scripture-loving, conscientious Jew. Though she lived among Christians, she knew almost as little of the Christian religion as if she had been an inhabitant of a heathen land.

She had many Christian customers, truly, but they spoke to her of needles and thread, and buttons and pins, with now and then a passing remark on the weather. They had never thought of winning the Jewess to a knowledge of the true Messiah. Naomi had been taught that it was a sin even to look into the New Testament, and she had no idea of its contents.

Knowing what were their mother's views, you will not be surprised to learn that Muppim and Huppim were growing up two as complete little Jews as could be found in our Christian land.

It was with regret that they saw Charlie Fay out with his sled and his ball on *their Sabbath*, and when on Sunday they peered at him through the window, as he passed on his way to Sunday-school, they wished he was a Jew like themselves. They could not bear to feel that there was any separation between them and their chosen friend.

By degrees, Muppim and Huppim were more and more in the shop, and at length, when they were eleven years old, it seemed given up to them almost entirely.

Naomi had work to do in the back room, that she could trust to no one else. She had another little black-eyed baby on her knee—a beautiful creature the twins thought him, and their father seemed much of the same opinion.

This baby Jacob called Ard, for, he said, having in his family the names of two of the sons of Benjamin, he meant to finish with a third. So "Muppim, Huppim, and Ard" were duly registered as the children of Jacob and Naomi Myers.

Now there was a new attraction for Charlie Fay at his next-door neighbor's. Charlie was the only son of his widowed mother, and the privilege of holding a baby was quite a novelty to him.

Charlie Fay seemed to have a natural talent for taking care of children, and when Ard would not stop crying for anything else, he would smile at the sight of Charlie, and be quite content if he could get his fingers fast among the little visitor's light curls.

So Charlie Fay grew more and more dear to Naomi, for she had a real mother's heart, and could be won through her children. With the apples for Muppim and Huppim, one was often placed for Charlie; and when winter came, Naomi knit, with her own hands, a warm tippet for the little neighbor, just like that worn by her own boys.

Naomi had never said to herself or to him that she loved Charlie Fay, *the Christian boy*, but he knew it, and she knew it. Though it had never been put into words, it had been told in a surer language.

IV.

Percussion Caps.

MANY and various were the trifling gifts the "little Jew boys" received from their mother's customers. The fact was, they were general favorites. One odd old gentleman often came to the shop, as much to talk to the children as to make purchases. He liked to puzzle the boys with queer questions, and hear their quick replies.

"Now, Muppim," said Mr. Thayer, one morning, "Now, Muppim, I've brought something to set you a thinking. If you will guess what these little bright boxes are for, I will give you—let me see—I will give you the whole case full of them!"

Mr. Thayer had on a rough suit of

clothes, and carried in his hand a bag which the boys well knew that he used when he made his trips to the country to hunt and fish for a few days.

"I want some strong twine," said the old gentleman, "and while you put me up a ball of it, you can have your thinking caps on."

The ball was promptly rolled up, and then Mr. Thayer said, "Well, Muppim, where's your answer?"

"I suppose," said the boy, "you use them when you go hunting; you put them on your gun, when it goes off!"

"Good! good! Did you ever see any before?" said the gentleman, clapping his hands.

"No, sir; but I've heard Charlie Fay tell about them, and he says its real fun to pound them, and hear them go off!"

"Dangerous sort of fun, I should think," said Mr. Thayer, "but you must have the percussion caps, Muppim. I'll warrant you'll sell them, and get a pretty price, too! The old gentleman placed the little box of caps in Muppim's hand, who looked up half-doubtingly, as if he perhaps ought not to accept them.

"Never fear, child; take them, they are fairly yours," said Mr. Thayer, leaving the shop.

"I'll give them to Charlie," said Muppim, with a bright smile on his face.

"And I'll see him crack them off!" said Huppim, joyously.

That afternoon, while the baby was asleep, Naomi went into the shop, and gave the boys liberty to go out for a little play. Their voices were no sooner heard on the pavement than they were joined by Charlie Fay.

Soon there was an ominous snapping and cracking, like the explosion of fire-arms. Naomi hastened to the door.

Charlie Fay was bending over the curb-stone, and was preparing to strike with a smoothing-iron he held in his hand, some bright little things that lay on the stone. The blow came down, and the next moment Charlie's screams filled the air, and his hands were pressed upon his eyes.

After this, Charlie Fay was not out on the pavement for many a day. The Doctor came and went from his mother's house, and Muppim and Huppim almost wept their eyes out, to hear that Charlie might be left blind by the accident.

Pieces of the percussion caps had entered his eyes, and it was feared that his sight was lost forever.

Naomi was surprised to find how deeply she was grieved. But for her shyness, she would have gone herself to inquire at the door for the poor little patient, and to express her sympathy for the mother. As it was, Muppim and Huppim were as regular in their appearance at Mrs. Fay's as the milk-man, at morning and evening.

They had never gained admittance, the sorrowful answer being always returned, that Charlie was no better.

One day, to their surprise, they were invited to walk in: "We must ask our mother first," said Muppim, doubtfully.

Naomi had never allowed her children to enter Mrs. Fay's house, or that of any other Christian, excepting upon necessary business; this, she thought, merely keeping them out of temptation.

Now the case seemed to her quite different. This was an act of mercy, like pulling a "neighbor's ox out of a pit—" there certainly could be no harm in this! Her loving heart yearned towards her fair-haired pet, her own Ard's pretty nurse.

Yet Naomi paused, and was silent for a moment, when the boys came in, eager with their request. She looked from one to the other, as if weighing their several capabilities, and then said, " I can trust you, Muppim, for five minutes ; but pray, as you cross the threshold, that the God of Israel will keep his own truth bright in your heart."

" I will, mother, I will," said Muppim, soberly. " I ought to go, for it was my fault that it all happened."

" It was Mr. Thayer's fault—Good Father Thayer, to blame you are! you had better take care, or Huppim Myers will put you in fires," said the other brother, with a laugh. " You go now, Muppim ; your solemncholy face will suit now, but when Charlie gets better, he'll want me, I tell you, to make him laugh."

" Very likely," said Muppim, quietly, as he went out the door.

Muppim did not forget his mother's precaution, as he entered the Christian's home.

Muppim was almost a stranger to Mrs. Fay. He had seen her from time to time at her door, and heard her kind voice speaking to her child, but a passing bow was all he had ever received from her.

Her black dress, and the signs of deep sorrow on her face, made the children associate something gloomy with her, and the twins had often wondered how Charlie could have so bright a face, when his mother was his only companion at home.

Now, Muppim expected to see Mrs. Fay more gloomy than ever, and he half dreaded a scolding from her, as he was really, in a measure, the cause of the accident.

The woman who had the lower floor of the house let Muppim in, and up stairs he went, finding his way to the door that was pointed out. His knock was soon answered.

"Why, Muppim! come in, dear," said

3*

Mrs. Fay, in a cheerful tone. "Charlie will be delighted to have you here."

"Muppim!" The voice called from the darkest corner of the room, where Charlie Fay was sitting, with a bandage over his eyes.

"Dear, dear Charlie," said Muppim, who was at his side, in a moment. "I am so sorry. Won't you ever see again?"

"Perhaps not!" said Charlie, very quietly.

"Oh! Charlie, don't say so!" said Muppim, taking both his friend's hands in his.

"I want to see again, of course," said Charlie, "but God will do for me just what is right."

Mrs. Fay slipped silently out of the room to hide her own tears, and the two boys were left together.

"What do you do when you are here, shut up?" said Muppim, trying to change the subject. "Sometimes mother reads to me; and when I am alone I say over hymns to myself; and then I know a great deal of Scripture, and I think about that. I say 'The Lord is my shepherd, I shall not want,' very often."

"Do you know that?" said Muppim, brightening.

"Yes, that is one of my favorites," said Charlie. "I like that part about 'I shall fear no evil.'"

Much as the two boys had been together, they had never spoken to each other of the deep religious earnestness that was alive in the hearts of both. Now they seemed suddenly united by a new bond.

Muppim found in Charlie a something which he had missed in his own brother. Together the twins studied their Scripture lessons and prayed, but with one it was a mere outward thing, while the other had felt that there was a solemn pleasure in anything that brought him near to God.

"Charlie," said Muppim, drawing close to his friend, "Charlie, I love you—we have missed you so! Mother says she wishes she could see you again, and Ard won't be still for anybody. Mother thinks he is fretting after you."

"The dear little chap!" said Charlie, warmly; "I should like to give him one toss-up.

"Why, Muppim! it makes me feel real well to have you here!"

"Then I'll come again very soon. I can't stay any longer now; mother only gave me five minutes."

"I see you keep up to 'honor thy father and thy mother,'" said Charlie, with a pleasant smile.

"That's my mark!" said Muppim, soberly. The text had been in his mind at the moment, as he was tempted to overstay the time his mother had allowed him for his visit.

Again he felt the new bond between him and his friend.

Ah, the Jews who train their children in the scriptures of the Old Testament, are preparing them for good things. It is the Jew who is lost in the love of gain, who insures for his children the curse pronounced on his doomed nation.

V.

Huppim's Visit.

ON the morning after Muppim's visit to Charlie Fay, Naomi and her children were in the "family-room," while Jacob, who chanced to be at home, was busy in the shop.

Huppim had been puffing out his cheeks and suddenly knocking them flat with his brown hands, while Ard's little face broke into pretty smiles at every explosion.

Muppim was poring over his father's copy of the Hebrew scriptures. He had found the twenty-third Psalm, and was trying to remember the exact English words in which Charlie Fay had translated it.

It was a new thing to Muppim to hear

scripture from a Christian's lips, and he had thought not a little about his interview of the day before. He had been taught that the Christians had a false Bible, and that their religion was a poor idolatry, to be dreaded and avoided by the Jews, the true people of God. Was Charlie, then, a Jew at heart? This question was in Muppim's mind, as he remembered the tone of real pleasure in which Charlie had spoken the sentence, " The Lord is my shepherd."

Muppim's meditations were suddenly disturbed by an unusual bound on the part of his brother, and the exclamation, " There, now! it is past 9 o'clock, and I want to be off to see Charlie Fay. May I, mother?"

Naomi had been deeply touched by Muppim's account of Charlie's gentleness and patience, and she had made up her mind that her boys should do all in their power to cheer him in his time of misfortune.

Now she laid aside her sewing quickly, and, taking out a worn purse from her pocket, she said, "Yes, Huppim, go comfort Charlie as well as you can, and take him an orange, too. Mind you make a good bargain, and don't stay more than half an hour."

Huppim took the pennies his mother held out to him, and was skipping away when a sudden thought struck him. "I'll carry in the buttons to sort; it will please Charlie, may be, to do it with me."

Naomi reached down the box of mixed buttons, and handed them to Huppim, who went off happy as a king.

Huppim's idea was a good one. Occupation was just what Charlie needed. He had borne up bravely so far, but now he must have company and employment. He must have that, even if his eyesight were not restored; he might be useful and cheerful.

Charlie was not above being pleased with the orange, and he thanked Huppim heartily for it, but the buttons were even more welcome. It was a pleasure to him to find out how readily he could distinguish the various kinds, by carefully examining them with his fingers, and at length he took the task of sorting them entirely upon himself, while Huppim sat by, sewing them diligently upon fresh blue papers, so as to make them look as they did when they were new.

"See, mother," said Charlie, with delight, "I can tell the porcelain ones in a moment from the horn ones. I have not made a single mistake yet, have I, Huppim?"

"You do it first-rate," said Huppim.

"Very nicely!" said the mother, in a low voice.

If Charlie had not been very busy about his work, he would have noticed the sad tones of his mother's voice.

Huppim gave him no chance for dwelling upon any thoughts just then, for he broke in, saying,—

"Suppose I tell you a story, Charlie; would you like it?"

"Indeed I should!" was the quick reply.

Huppim began, much as if he was reading from a book, "Rabbi Hillel was a very meek man. One day somebody made a bet that no one could make the Rabbi angry. One fellow came to the Rabbi, when he was in a hurry getting ready for the Sabbath, and asked him a great many foolish questions, enough to put any body out of patience; but the Rabbi, instead of getting angry, answered every one in the pleasantest way in the world. So this fellow did not make out.

Then another thought he would try; so he came to the Rabbi, and said, 'Can you teach me the whole law during the time I can stand on one foot?' 'Yes,' said the Rabbi, 'for the whole law is in this short sentence, "Whatever you would not wish your neighbor to do to you, do it not to him." This is the whole law.' Was not that a smart answer?"

"It was so!" said Charlie, warmly. "I think that Rabbi was a remarkable man. If anything puts me out of patience, it is being questioned when I am in a hurry."

"Then you ought not to have Mr. Thayer to deal with. He's the one for questions!" said Huppim.

The clock here struck out plainly. Huppim jumped. "I declare," he said, "I have been here ever so many minutes more than mother said, so I must be off in a twinkling. I'll leave the buttons, Charlie!"

"Yes, do! and tell Muppim I want to see him."

Huppim answered "Ay! ay!" from the stair-way, as he went bounding down three steps at a time.

Mrs. Fay closed the door, and sat down beside her boy.

"Mother," he said, as he laid his head on her shoulder, "Mother, I may be able to be of some use to you, even if I am blind. I mean to try to learn to do all I can, and then I shall not be a burden to you."

Charlie spoke cheerfully, but the words went straight home like a pang to his mother's heart.

"I do not believe you are to be blind, my own dear boy," she said, while the tears filled her eyes to overflowing. "I do not let myself think of that as possible."

"But I do, mother; and somehow, I

think God is going to answer in this way a prayer I have made night and morning for a long time. I have asked God to let me be very useful in this world, and teach a great many people to love him. I think I wanted to do great things ; and perhaps he is going to let me be useful, but make me blind, too, to keep me humble."

Mrs. Fay bowed down beside the bed, and prayed and wept in silence.

Had not she, too, been full of pride in her noble boy? Had not she, too, thought of the " great things" he would do in the world, and of the praise he would win from men ?

When Mrs. Fay rose from her knees, it was to kiss Charlie very tenderly, and to say to him, " We will not talk about the future, darling, we have only to bear our present trials. You will be happier to be occupied now, and it will do you no harm, whether you see again or not. We know that God will arrange all things in the best way."

Charlie broke forth singing the hymn,

> "God moves in a mysterious way,"

and when he came to the lines,

> "The bud may have a bitter taste,
> But sweet will be the flower,"

so beautiful a smile passed over his face, that his mother felt that she could already see the blessed effects of his affliction, and thenceforward would stifle every murmur.

She had prayed that her son might be a faithful, useful follower of Jesus, and she would have the Lord answer her prayers in his own wise way.

VI.

The Dreaded Name.

NAOMI had given her promise that one of the boys should visit Charlie each day, and they peaceably agreed to take turns, as their mother could not well spare them both at once.

When Muppim prepared for his interview the next day, he was careful to take with him the Hebrew Scriptures, with a mark put in at the twenty-third Psalm.

"You are going to read to Charlie; that is kind," said Mrs. Fay, noticing the book.

"I can only read Hebrew; mother did not care to have us learn to read English," said Muppim, shyly.

"Read me some Hebrew—I should so

like to hear the sound of it," said Charlie, eagerly. There was something delightful to Charlie in the idea of hearing even a few words of that ancient language spoken by Moses and the prophets.

"You must wait until I go out, before you begin such learned proceedings," said Mrs. Fay, with a smile. "How long can you stay, Muppim?"

"A whole hour to-day, mother says," was Muppim's joyous answer.

"Then, Charlie, I shall take a walk, and attend to all my business for the day," said the mother.

The boys had some pleasant chat while Mrs. Fay was making her preparations, but as soon as she closed the door, Charlie broke out, "Now for the reading, Muppim."

Muppim read aloud the twenty-third Psalm, and as he closed, before Charlie could speak, he said, "Say what you did yesterday, Charlie, 'The Lord is my shepherd.'"

Charlie repeated the whole Psalm, while Muppim followed him in the Hebrew, with his finger passing along the page, and his eye full of delight. "It is just the same; just the same as I have it here! Do you know any more, Charlie?"

Charlie recited the 103d and the 51st Psalms, while Muppim looked over, with the same pleasure as before.

"Do you like the Jews, Charlie?" asked Muppim, abruptly.

"Indeed I do—I would rather be a Jew than belong to any other nation," said Charlie, warmly.

Muppim took his friend's hand, and looked eagerly into his face. Charlie's speaking eyes were hidden from sight; he could not see Muppim's searching, questioning gaze, nor could Muppim find his answer in his companion's tranquil countenance.

"I love the Jews, and mother loves them, too," said Charlie.

Muppim was silent for a moment, and then he said, suddenly, "Can you say the Ten Commandments?"

Charlie repeated them slowly and reverently, as he had been taught to recite the word of God; and as he finished, he said, "I learned those when I was a little bit of a boy, Muppim; and I say them over every night, and try to think whether I have broken any of them."

"Of course you don't break any of them, but may-be the tenth," said Muppim.

"I mean whether I have broken them in my heart," said Charlie, soberly.

"If you break a commandment, how dare you go to sleep?" said Muppim, with his eyes wide open; "I always feel as if something dreadful would carry me off, as the devil came after Rabbi ben Rikel's son, when he fell asleep at his prayers."

"I am not afraid to go to sleep, because I ask pardon for the sake of the Lord Jesus," said Charlie.

Muppim started up suddenly, and repeating the prayer, that "The Lord would keep His truth bright in his heart," the young Jew hurried from the room. He had made up his mind never to hear the name of Jesus mentioned, so he should be sure to keep out of temptation. Charlie was for a few moments puzzled to understand Muppim's sudden departure, but at length he guessed the true reason. Charlie was not lonely during the half-hour that passed before his mother returned; he was too busily occupied in mind to think of loneliness, or time. He was praying, oh, how earnestly! for his Jewish friends, and asking wisdom to guide them into the knowledge of Jesus, the true Messiah.

VII.

The Playfellows' Meeting.

MUPPIM took his Hebrew Bible no more to Charlie Fay's. He had no more talks with him about Psalms or Commandments. Yet the twins were faithful in their visits to the little prisoner. Huppim was most ingenious in finding occupation for Charlie; he had twine to untangle, and twine to be rolled up; indeed, the shop was always sure to yield some work to be done, when Huppim went to pass his hour with the patient boy. Huppim was full of out-door life, and stories of out-door fun; he had a store of anecdotes laid up of what he had seen in the street, to amuse Charlie; and then Ard's baby-ways were always certain to interest his old playfellow.

Ard, meanwhile, was coming on finely. Although he chose not to use his sturdy legs for walking, he could creep about the floor so fast as to wear off the toes of a pair of new shoes in a week, and his little teeth were sharp enough to leave their marks on everything they touched, as Naomi's baby-spoon showed very plainly. Ard was talking more and more, too, and Huppim thought it would do Charlie real good to hear him; Mrs. Fay thought so too, and so Ard was brought in one day, by his merry brother, to pay Charlie a visit. A great clumsy bundle, done up in a shawl, he seemed, as he was deposited on the floor to be unrolled. Then out came the fattest, brownest, most dark-eyed little fellow Mrs. Fay had ever seen.

"Ard! Ard! don't you know me!" said Charlie, stooping down tenderly beside the child. The sturdy boy pushed Charlie back with his stout hands, and said, "Way, way! way, way!"

Charlie put his arm round the little fellow, and began to sing, in a cheerful voice, a lively tune, of which Ard had been very fond.

The child looked up wonderingly, and then, with a sudden movement, snatched the bandage from Charlie's eyes.

"Do you know Charlie, now?" said the poor boy.

Ard made no answer, but nestled contentedly beside his old friend.

"Oh! you seem like yourself, now!" exclaimed Huppim. A sad smile passed over Charlie's face, and he dropped his lids till the long lashes lay on his pale cheeks.

"Let me see your eyes," said Huppim, who was not troubled with any particular delicacy of feeling.

"They are quite healed now, and the doctor says they will be better without the bandage," said Mrs. Fay, quietly. "Ard has helped us to carry out the good doctor's prescription."

Charlie had shrunk from taking off the bandage. While it covered his eyes he could fancy that its folds kept out the light; he feared, too, that his sightless eyes would give pain to all who looked upon him, and draw forth disgust as well as pity.

His mother knew that one who had so meekly bowed to the will of Heaven when blindness was sent him, would not long be ruled by such a little weakness, and she had gently let him have his way.

Ard's busy hands had come in to do what the mother had left for time.

For a few moments Charlie sat silent and with downcast eyes, after Huppim's abrupt expression of his wish.

Those few moments were spent in prayer. Charlie asked to be enabled to take with cheerful submission every circumstance connected with his misfortune; then he was ready to lift those long lashes, and to show his sightless eyes to his friend.

There was nothing in that exhibition to shock the most sensitive of beings, and Huppim by no means belonged to that class.

"Why, they don't look badly a bit, Charlie! They are just as blue as ever, and only have a little white spot where the black one used to be, in the middle. Why, it don't seem as if you could be blind! I never saw your face when I liked it half as well!" said Huppim, with surprise in his tones.

Mrs. Fay had listened anxiously to the first part of his speech, fearing its effect upon her dear boy; but Charlie was stayed upon a rock! There was truly an expression upon his young face which beautified him in his blindness!

The mother drew near, and kissed him tenderly as she said, "I have no fears for you now, my son! God will sustain you, and make you useful and beloved."

"Heaven will seem all the more beautiful to me, when I come out of this darkness!" said Charlie, as he leaned his head against his mother. "I never felt happier in my life, and you were never half so dear to me. God has helped me to bear this trial, and all seems bright to me now."

Ard's little hand was passed tenderly down Charlie's cheek at that moment, and, as if a forgotten tune had suddenly come to his mind, the child murmured "Char-char—Char-char," so lovingly, that Charlie stooped down to kiss him, and hugged him close in his arms.

Huppim gave a full account of that visit

at the dinner-table that day. Not a word or look had escaped his observing eyes. Charlie Fay had given a testimony to the truth of the Christian faith, which was not soon to be forgotten in the Jewish home.

VIII.

Purim at Jacob Myers'.

MARCH had come, with its blue skies and blustering winds. The Jews counted themselves in the twelfth month of their sacred year, and now the feast of Purim was to be kept. This is a feast of two days, in which the Jews remember the time when their nation was saved from destruction by the courage and resolution of Queen Esther. Ever since Haman was hanged, and Mordecai was raised to honor, the feast of Purim has been kept among the Jews, as it was at first,—a time "of feasting and joy, and of sending portions one to another, and gifts to the poor."

You will find the account of the origin of these days in the book of Esther, one of the most interesting of the Old Testament stories.

There was a busy time at Jacob Myers' before the feast of Purim. Each member of the family had gifts to prepare for the others, and all was done with the greatest secrecy.

Muppim and Huppim consulted as to what should be prepared for Naomi. They wanted to give their present together, to their mother. They felt, that at such a time, twins should not be separate, but it was hard for them to agree. Huppim's taste was quite for the practical. He thought a new saucepan, such as he had heard her wishing for, would be a most acceptable gift.

Muppim, meanwhile, was in favor of some pots of early flowers, from a neighboring greenhouse, to place in her sunny south window. He was sure they would please his mother best, and besides, he had a kind of a notion that they would speak his feelings better than a saucepan.

Muppim had his own way in this, as he generally did, for he had the stronger will of the two, and besides, managed to give Huppim a wonderful idea of his superior judgment.

Perhaps you wonder where the twins got their money for their purchases. The young Jews had not lived to be nearly thirteen years old, without making many bargains of their own, and earning many a penny. True, they brought all their gains to their mother, but she kept them apart from her own, and duly made of them a private purse that was to be theirs when they were older. Now, however, they had liberty to keep, for a week or two, whatever they might make in their various transactions.

They did not have to stay many mornings about the steamboat landings before they had an opportunity of earning a few sixpences with which to begin, and then, such trade as they knew how to manage in oranges, apples, cigars, pins and matches helped them out with their fund for Purim.

The feast days came in due time, and Jacob was in the city, to go to the synagogue to hear the story of Esther read, and to cry, "let his name be blotted out," whenever Haman was mentioned. That was not, however, the part of the proceedings which pleased Jacob best. He was happier when he had Ard on his knee, crowing and rejoicing in his own way over his new playthings, and beating his gaily-painted drum, till nothing else could be heard in the room.

The perfume of the flowers was sweet to Naomi, and in the midst of her thanks Muppim gave a look of triumph at his brother, which said very plainly, "You see, I knew what would please mother best." Huppim bowed in submission; he was too well satisfied with his new knife and the marbles in his pockets, to be out of humor about anything. We cannot give all the proceedings of those days of rejoicing, we cannot tell all the good things that Naomi had prepared, or with what relish they were eaten, nor of the poor, half-starved Jews who that day had a share of Naomi's nice cooking.

Charlie Fay, too, came in for his portion of his neighbors' joy. True, he was not a Jew, and had no right to partake of a Jewish feast, but Muppim and Huppim could not have had their hearts glad, without knowing that the blind boy had some new cause of pleasure. Even Naomi herself would not have felt quite satisfied, unless Charlie had been in some way included in their merry-making.

There could certainly be no harm in remembering one so afflicted, at such a time, even if he were not a Jew.

So Charlie had a box of fresh mignonette, that filled his room with perfume which rose with his prayers that his neighbors might some day know the true joy that is only found in Christ Jesus.

But Muppim—had he no share in the general rejoicing? He was not much given to merry-making, and of late he had been particularly thoughtful, yet there was a look of hearty gratification in his face, as he held in his hand the book that had been given him.

All the family had joined their funds to purchase Muppim's present, a copy of the Hebrew Scriptures; though his father did not much approve of the proceeding. He thought it was well, of course, to be regular at the Synagogue, and to be particular as to Jewish feasts and ceremonies, but Muppim had a way of studying the

Scriptures that Jacob deemed in his heart but little better than a waste of time. Naomi, however, was too good a wife to be opposed in a plan against which no plausible objection could be urged, especially as Jacob had a point of his own to carry before he left home again.

There *was* something peculiar in Muppim's study of the Scriptures. Few of the Jews of our day care as much even for the revered Old Testament as for their own sacred writers of the Talmud. There are a dozen who know the fables of that composition of men, for one who is well versed in the Old Testament history, the soul-searching Psalms, or the sublime prophesies of Isaiah. Muppim had caught his mother's reverence for the inspired word of God, and now he was spurred on to its study by a new motive.

On the first moment of retirement that was his, after the reception of the gift, he stood alone in his chamber, and solemnly said, as he laid his hand on his book, "Bring us back, O our Father, to the observance of thy law, and make us to adhere to thy precepts; and do thou, O our King, draw us near to thy worship, and convert us to thee by perfect repentance in thy presence. Blessed art thou, O Lord, who vouchsafest to receive us by repentance.

"Thou of thy mercy givest knowledge unto men, and teachest them understanding; give graciously unto me knowledge, wisdom, and understanding. Blessed art thou, O Lord, who graciously givest knowledge unto men."

These prayers Muppim spoke in the Hebrew language, in which they were first written and have been used for hundreds of years,—some say, since before the time of our Saviour's appearance on earth. The eighteen peculiarly precious prayers of the Jews, of which these are two, Muppim had heard at the Synagogue worship, and three times a day he had *said* them in private, yet he had never *prayed* in those time-honored words before. He had never so longed to understand God's truth.

IX.

The Old Gentleman.

LITTLE by little Jacob Myers was adding to his gains and enlarging his business. He felt that in this country there was nothing in the way of an industrious man, and that even a Jew might rise to great prosperity and influence. Not that Jacob was particularly ambitious for himself,—his present way of life suited him very well,—but he had sons coming forward, and it was of them and of their future he frequently thought.

His mind often travelled on to the time when the sign "Muppim and Huppim Myers" should grace one of the largest establishments in the city, and the wealthy owners have the respect and esteem of the rich and poor. Jacob well knew that all this could not be brought about without much care, labor, and painstaking, and he felt that he had latterly been losing time. His boys were not preparing for the position he coveted for them.

Upon one thing Jacob was resolved. Muppim and Huppim must learn to read English, and know something more of arithmetic than they had already learned in the shop.

From Naomi he expected much opposition to his new proposal, and he therefore announced it to her as a matter already settled, merely saying that he should spend the Sundays, when he was necessarily at home, in teaching his children to read English, and he should like to have them prepare themselves during the week, and make as rapid progress as possible.

Naomi submitted, like a true wife, in silence, but she inwardly trembled at the temptation her children would be exposed to, in having the power to read all the bad books which she had been told were printed in English. She rejoiced that the time was near when her twins, according to the Jewish view, would be of an age to account for their own actions, for she sadly feared they would go far astray.

Hard would it be for parents, if all the sins of children under thirteen were to be visited upon them. The holy Scriptures even of the Old Testament give us another rule, "The soul that sinneth it shall die."

Muppim received with joy his father's announcement. He was eager for all knowledge, and was just now particularly anxious to be able to read English for a private reason of his own.

Huppim, on the contrary, expressed his pity for his father, if he expected to teach him, and declared his belief that both would give up in despair before many weeks were over.

The brothers were busy with their spelling-books, behind the counter, one day, when an unexpected customer came in.

The boys started with pleasure.

"So you do know me!" said Mr. Thayer. "Why haven't you been to look me up? Didn't you know I'd been sick? I've been almost a dead man, and neither of you so much as came to see if I was alive! Don't you feel ashamed of yourselves?"

"Not a bit of it. But I am sorry you have been sick," said Huppim.

"I did not know where you lived. I wondered what had become of you," said Muppim.

"You sha'n't say that again. Here's my address. John Thayer,—there's the street and number and all," said the old gentleman, placing his card on the counter. "Take it, Muppim, you are the steadiest. My friend Huppim, there, wouldn't mind winding a fishing-line on it, if he were in a hurry. Now, if I ever go six months without stopping in here again, you may conclude I'm sick, and come to look after me. I have no boys of my own, but if I am a bachelor I can have my fancies. I like young faces, and should have been mighty glad to see you when I was shut up there by myself. I found plenty to think about, though, and may-be I'll tell you about that some other time."

"I'll take care of the card, and not forget what you say," said Muppim, as he put the card away in his own little pocket-book.

"What are you doing there? That don't look like Hebrew," said Mr. Thayer, glancing at the spelling-book.

"We are learning to read English,"

was Muppim's answer, and his tone proved that he did not think it a disagreeable announcement.

"The very thing! Just what I was wishing!" said Mr. Thayer, with surprise. "Well, we are short-sighted mortals, actually blind."

"Have you heard about Charlie Fay?" asked Muppim, reminded by Mr. Thayer's last word, of his afflicted friend.

"What! your curly-headed playfellow? No harm has come to him, I hope."

"It was all my fault, after your telling me cracking off the caps was dangerous fun," began Muppim; and then he went on to tell the story of Charlie's accident, and his patience under his sore trial.

"I must go and see him this very minute," said Mr. Thayer; "I was to blame to trust you boys with such things, just for a whim, without more of a warning. Show me where he lives,—I'll go and see him!"

Muppim pointed out the house, and was about to enter with Mr. Thayer, but the old gentleman stopped him, saying, " No, no, Muppim! go back to your books; I'll see Charlie by myself. I don't care to have you see an old fellow like me make himself foolish. Why, the idea of that fine little chap's losing his eyes makes a baby of me."

Mr. Thayer's knock was answered by Mrs. Fay.

" I want to see Charlie Fay all alone," said Mr. Thayer, quickly.

" You can do so, sir, if you will walk up stairs," said Mrs. Fay, leading the way to her humble apartments.

" Charlie, there is a gentleman here who wishes to see you," said the mother, as she opened the door.

Charlie was sitting at a small table, busily tracing with his fingers the embossed patterns on some papers from the wrappings to linen. As his eyes were cast down, his was as noble a young head as one would wish to see. He involuntarily raised his lashes at the entrance of a stranger, but it was to realize no change in his darkness.

"Charlie, my boy, do you remember Mr. Thayer?" said the old gentleman.

Charlie could not forget that name; it was too deeply associated with his misfortune.

"Yes, sir, I remember you," he quietly answered. "You used to stop often to buy of Mrs. Myers, and talk to the boys."

"Charlie," said Mr. Thayer, very tenderly, "Charlie, I would rather have lost these old eyes, than have been the means of having this happen to you. I have a great deal to account for in my life. I have had enough to think about on my sick-bed, but I did not know I had *this* to lie at my door, for my foolishness."

"Don't blame yourself, sir. My misfortune was sent to me by my Heavenly Father, and I believe He meant it for my good," said Charlie. "You could not know what Muppim would do with the caps. I believe it is going to turn out for the good of us all. Muppim and Huppim have been a great deal to see me. They are very kind. Oh, sir, I do wish they were Christians!"

"And so do I!" said Mr. Thayer, taking Charlie's hand, quickly; "I thought of that on my sick-bed. My boy, I thought of a great deal I had forgotten all my life. You ought to be thankful that you have found your Heavenly Father in your youth. Thanks be unto Him, He receives the old when they repent, but He cannot make them forget the past."

"Yet He forgives all the past, so we need not think about it," said Charlie.

"No! That is true. And I mean to

keep so busy that I shall have no time to dwell on what I ought to have done long ago. About Muppim and Huppim I felt quite desperate, but here, as soon as I get about, I find them learning English; then what is to prevent their studying the Bible, and being made true Christians?"

"That is what I pray for every day, and I think it will be so," said Charlie, cheerfully. "Muppim won't talk to me any more even about the Old Testament, but I know he reads it every day, and that is the best thing, just now. Mother says he could not do better than read the Old Testament faithfully, and then he will be more sure to see that our Saviour is the real Messiah."

Mr. Thayer looked at Charlie's young face, so full of interest for his friends, and felt the beauty of the early love of the truth, before the world and its cares have left but half a heart to be given to God.

"We will not give up our little Jews," said Mr. Thayer; "but, Charlie, I want to do something for you. Is there no way in which I can oblige you?"

"I am used to living plainly, and we have every comfort," said Charlie, "and my own dear mother—nobody could be sweeter and kinder than she is. Thank you, Mr. Thayer, I do not need anything but more patience and cheerfulness, and my Best Friend will give them, if I ask Him, and try myself."

"Charlie, I want to see more of you; may I come again and sit awhile with you to-morrow?" said Mr. Thayer. He felt that as he was now in the heavenly path, he might learn much from this dear child of God.

"Do come,—I like to have company," said Charlie; "and I am so glad that you are interested about Muppim and Huppim, —interested, I mean, as I am."

"Charlie," said Mr. Thayer, taking both the blind boy's hands in his own, "Charlie, I want everybody to feel as I do. God has forgiven me, when I so little deserve it, and I want every one to turn to Him, and find how full of love and mercy He is."

"How I love to hear you say so!" said Charlie. "Something pleasant seems to be happening for me all the while, now that I am blind."

As Mr. Thayer walked away from that humble home, he felt more than ever the power and beauty of the Christian religion. Charlie Fay had early begun to walk in wisdom's ways of "pleasantness," or he would not have found cause for thankfulness as he sat in his darkness, cut off from all the pleasures of boyhood.

X.

The Reward-Card.

MR. THAYER had been an active, successful merchant. Through his long life he had done heartily whatever he had undertaken. He was not now going to make a listless, do-nothing Christian, if there are any such who deserve the name of Christians. Mr. Thayer meant to work, and work heartily in his Master's service.

Before he slept, after his interview with Charlie Fay, he had hit upon a plan for his daily amusement and improvement.

The next morning Mr. Thayer's cane sounded on the wide stone walk that led up to the door of the Blind Asylum, in his native city. Before many hours were over, he had gone through the Institution, and engaged a place for a new pupil. Who that pupil was to be, will readily be guessed.

Charlie's face lighted up with a perfect glow of pleasure when the plan was proposed to him, but the glow faded away, as he said, " I know where the Asylum is—I have often passed it. It is too far for mother to walk every day, and I cannot go alone."

Mr. Thayer looked puzzled for a moment, and then he answered, " We will see what Muppim and Huppim will say about that."

Muppim, Huppim, and Naomi were all of one mind upon the subject. The twins could well be spared to go with Charlie to school, and call for him at noon when the study hours were over. His work he could do at home. Yes—" work." He was to be taught how to make baskets and mats, to knit and to crochet, as well as to read with his fingers' ends.

A new life now opened before Charlie Fay. Every morning he had a walk in the fresh air with his two friends, and daily they learned more of his patient, cheerful spirit.

Muppim thought how discontent would have crept over him, if he had been tried with the loss of his precious sight; and Huppim felt sure he, in like circumstances, would have given up in despair.

The twins had never thought of being grateful for the common blessings of life,—health and strength, food and clothing,—but Charlie seemed welling over with gratitude for the many comforts and sources of pleasure still left to him.

Muppim had ceased to talk with Charlie of religion, but he could not fail to notice the sweet joyousness of this dear follower of Jesus, and in the young Jew there was an increasing questioning interest as to the possible truth of the Christian's faith. This had spurred him on to a faithful study of the Old Testament; for this he now longed to read the New. Yet he thought, and studied, and prayed in silence. Not even his twin brother, or his tender, loving mother guessed the thoughts that were agitating his mind. But there was one more loving than a mother, more faithful than a brother, who was watching with tender interest the workings of Muppim's heart, and yearning for this child of Israel to turn unto Him.

Charlie had been a week at the Blind Asylum, when he received a card of reward for good behavior. A perfect treasure this card was for him, for it was printed with the letters raised, so that he could feel them as he slowly passed his fingers over them, and so practise his new way of learning to read.

Charlie, of course, had made but little progress as yet, in this method of reading. Like most boys, he had put his hands through a hardening process in his plays, not to speak of the work he had done in his anxiety to assist his mother. But for the time he had spent in his darkened room, his fingers would have been stiff and clumsy enough, and even now they would need much and thorough training before they would serve him instead of eyes.

To the twins Charlie's card was a real curiosity. They had never heard of the way of teaching the blind to read, by using raised letters, and they were full of wonder and interest about it.

"Let me try," said Huppim, stopping in the street to pass his horny fingers' ends along the page.

"I should never learn to read that way," he said with a laugh. "I can only feel a little roughness, and no shape of the letters at all."

Muppim, of course, tried the experiment too, and with no better success.

"Perhaps you could not read it, even by looking at it," said Charlie. "I don't know what it says myself. The teacher wouldn't tell me; he wanted me to find out. You boys can read it, and then you can see how I make out."

Muppim forthwith went through a great deal of spelling, as he walked slowly along, but as he had only been at his English studies three weeks, he made a poor hand at deciphering it.

"I'll get mother to read it to you," said Charlie, "and then you can try me every day, and see how I get on."

Mrs. Fay was glad to hear the boys talking so cheerfully as they came up the stairs. She readily promised to give the secret of the card to the young Jews, while Charlie stopped on the landing, and put his fingers into his ears lest he should hear more than was fair, under the circumstances. The words on the card were very familiar to Mrs. Fay—she needed but a glance to be able to speak them all; yet Muppim and Huppim listened again and again, as she went over with them, that they might catch at least a single sentence and keep it in memory.

"Our Father who art in Heaven," she began, and so through the Lord's prayer she went, while the Jews followed, little thinking that they were speaking the words of Jesus. Yet, there was a charm to Muppim in that prayer. Huppim had remembered but the mere beginning of it. That, he said, would be enough for the present; he could learn more when Charlie was able to make out the first sentence. When Muppim's hour of evening prayer came, "Our Father who art in Heaven" was suggested to his mind, and he went on till he came to "forgive us our trespasses as we forgive those who trespass against us." The idea and the words were puzzling to him; here he stopped.

Muppim could not be content to half learn anything. He was not satisfied until Mrs. Fay had read to him what was on the card, again and again, and he was able to repeat the very words. Charlie, meanwhile, spent many a minute passing his fingers over the letters,—as yet, in vain. The time was not lost; Muppim was taking home the words to his heart. We cannot say that he prayed in them, but when he stood at his prayers, they came into his mind, and he began, as a habit, to try himself upon them when he had finished his own petitions.

Jesus, who "saw Jerusalem and wept over it," does not forget his own nation now; gladly does he welcome each sign that a Jew is turning his face towards the true Canaan, and is preparing to acknowledge Zion's King.

When we pray for the Jews, when we labor to lead them to Christ, we are sharing His spirit who would have saved them from destruction, "but they would not," and who, even now, "waiteth to be gracious" to His "own brethren according to the flesh," as well as to the multitude of the Gentiles.

XI.

The Passover.

CHARLIE FAY was surprised one morning by an early visit from Huppim. "I have brought you a present, Charlie," said the young Jew: "here is one of mother's good loaf-cakes; she sent it to you with her love."

"Thank you, twenty times," said Charlie, feeling the weight of the cake with his hands; "but had not we boys better halve it? A part of it would last mother and me ever so long."

"Not a morsel of it can we have on our premises: why, it is raised cake, and to-night father is to search the house to see that there is not a bit of leaven in it. Mother don't want him to find so much as a crumb of leavened bread to cast out," said Huppim.

"What, has the Passover come so soon? It don't seem to me as if it was a month since Purim," said Charlie, who had become familiar with the seasons for celebrating the Jewish feasts.

"But it is, though," said Huppim; "to-morrow is the fourteenth day of the first month, and of course we are to keep the Passover. Oh! I forgot; here's the spring-beer mother sent you and Mrs. Fay,—the last bottle of that, too; she says it is strengthening, and you know we don't have anything of that kind in our house at Passover time."

Charlie thought of the Saviour's command to put away all the leaven of evil out of the heart, and wondered when his dear Jewish friends would understand the spiritual meaning of the ceremonies they observed so carefully. He contented himself with a prayer for them, without any attempt to teach them, at that time, the true way. He knew that at present any direct efforts on his part would prevent his young friends from visiting him any more, and so deprive him of all possibility of influencing them : he must watch, and pray, and wait, and in the Lord's good time, he doubted not, they would be brought to the knowledge of Jesus.

Charlie Fay meant to keep the Passover with his friends, in his own way; he got his mother to read over to him the eleventh, twelfth, and thirteenth chapters of Exodus, where the account is given of the origin of this great feast of the Jews.

The Passover is kept in memory of the time when the angel of the Lord passed over the houses of the Israelites when he slew the first-born in every house of the Egyptians. At that time the Lord commanded His people to keep the Passover *forever*, and told them that this time should be to them the beginning of months, the first month in the year. Even now, the month of the Passover is to the Jews the beginning of their religious year, though it is in our spring.

This year the Passover came in April. It was Nisan or Abib with the Jews, but April to all Christians. When Charlie heard the account of the sacrifice of the lamb in the Passover, he wondered whether his friends would offer up a lamb, and was surprised to think he had never looked to see if there was blood on their door-posts at the Passover time. Through all the day Charlie was dwelling upon the Passover time as it is described in Scripture. His mother read to him how Jesus kept the feast with His disciples, and then how He Himself suffered on the cross, to be the true Lamb slain for our sins, that we might have free forgiveness.

Meanwhile, preparations were going on at Jacob Myers' for the proper ceremonies of the evening; not a member of the family had eaten a mouthful, excepting little Ard, who had been as industrious in that way as usual.

The rest of the household had joined in the prayers of the synagogue, Jacob and Huppim with their lips alone, but Naomi and Muppim with their hearts as well as their mouths. When evening was come, three plates were set upon the table;—one plate contained three Passover cakes, looking very much like large, hard sea-biscuit. These cakes had been made up quickly, without yeast or leaven of any kind; the three cakes were carefully laid one above another, in a napkin.

The second plate had in it horse-radish and bitter herbs. The third plate contained a small bone of lamb and a roasted egg.

Besides the three plates, there were two dishes, one of which was filled with vinegar and salt, and the other with a mixture somewhat like lime. There was a wine-glass for each member of the family.

Several Hebrew blessings were repeated, then the first cup of wine was drunk.

Jacob then dipped some of the bitter herbs in the vinegar, and gave a small portion to his wife and to each of the boys. After that, he broke the middle one of the three cakes, and hid away half of it until after supper.

Then all the family put their hands upon the dishes containing the Passover cakes and the bitter herbs and said, " Lo, this is the bread of affliction, which our fathers ate in the land of Egypt ; let all those who are hungry come and eat thereof, and all who are needy come and celebrate our Passover. At this time we are here ; next year we hope to be in the land of Israel: now we are servants; next year we hope to be free children."

Muppim and Huppim then asked, " Wherefore is this night distinguished from all other nights?"

To which their parents replied, " Because we were slaves unto Pharaoh in Egypt, and the Lord our God brought us out from thence, with a mighty hand and a stretched out arm."

Jacob then read the account of the wonders God wrought for His people of Israel, and the mother and children made answer from time to time on the same subject.

To each a piece of the unleavened bread was then given, and some of the bitter herbs, dipped in the mixture like lime, was eaten by all.

Then followed the setting of various good things on the table. Ard was helped up to his high-chair, and made up, by his merry ways, for his quiet behavior during the service just performed.

There was but a small family at the feast, but it seemed a happy one, and as Naomi looked about her, she wondered if there were in all the country three as promising boys as her own.

The family feast being over, Jacob poured out two cups of wine; one of them Jacob took, and then said solemnly, "O Most Merciful! make us to inherit the day when all shall be Sabbath, and we shall rest in life forever. O Most Merciful! make us worthy to see the days of the Messiah, and life in the world to come."

Other words of like kind followed, and then Jacob gave the cup to each of the family, and to each a piece of the hidden unleavened bread, which he had before taken from the table.*

The second cup of wine, called by the

---

* Read carefully St. Luke xxii, 19, 20.

Jews Elijah's cup, " the cup after supper," he then placed before him; the boys opened the door, and there was a time of silence and solemn expectation. All looked eagerly out, hoping to see Elijah entering to announce that the true Messiah was coming. No old prophet rose from the dead to tell them that the Messiah, the Saviour of the world, had already come and had been crucified; but as the Jewish family sat there in solemn silence, a sound of music floated in through the open door; —Charlie Fay's sweet voice was heard in the hymn—

> "Come, let us sing of Jesus,
>   While hearts and accents blend;
> Come, let us sing of Jesus,
>   The sinner's only Friend."

To Muppim, this seemed like a message from heaven. Was not this Jesus, whom Charlie Fay so loved, the Messiah? The question sank deep into the heart of the young Jew.

Charlie Fay was but singing his evening hymn, after his happy day of drawing near to his Lord. He had felt more than ever the blessedness of knowing Him who is the only sacrifice for sin, and the true Lamb of the Passover.

When this hymn was over, Charlie knelt down for his evening prayers;—not for himself alone he prayed, but for his dear friends, and particularly for all the Jews, who were then keeping the Passover in darkness and unbelief.

Meanwhile, Jacob Myers' family were closing their solemn feast by singing an ancient hymn, beginning, "Lord, build Thy temple speedily."

Even as these words were in his ears, Muppim, in his heart, was repeating, "Come, let us sing of Jesus," and longing to know more of that Jesus, of whom Charlie Fay was a follower.

Charlie Fay had not argued with his Jewish friends, but he had been doing more for his religion; Charlie had been showing forth cheerfulness in affliction, and an unselfish, lovely spirit, which they could not but admire. The thoughtful Muppim was beginning to question what could be the power that so sustained Charlie in his time of trial, and made him so gentle and kindly in daily life.

Ah! faithful living is a safe kind of teaching. Children *may* go astray when they strive to give advice; but a single mild, forgiving, truthful, obedient Christian child is doing much for the religion of Jesus. She is a true missionary to all her companions, and many will wish to follow her Lord.

If all Christians were such as they should be, then would the Jews be forced to say, The Messiah must have come ; for behold, here is a people who walk in God's laws and keep His commandments better than we ; they must have been taught by the Son of David ; their Lord must be the King of the Jews!

XII.

Beginnings.

MUPPIM and Huppim were now thirteen years of age, and with the usual ceremonies, they had taken their position as full worshippers at the synagogue, and according to Jewish belief were persons accountable for their own lives.

Huppim felt very proud on the occasion; he seemed to think himself now a man, and of course much wiser than any woman. It was quite amusing to see the important air of the young Jew, puffed up with his new dignity. If Huppim had had a better knowledge of his own heart, he would have seen more cause for humility than for pride in his present position.

To be accountable for one's own sins is certainly an awful, solemn thought; yet this is true of every one of us!

Muppim, meanwhile, had a secret cause of anxiety that made him more thoughtful than ever. One question had taken deep hold of his mind, "What if the religion of the Christian should be true, and Messiah be already come?"

How he longed to talk with Charlie about the subject that was ever in his mind! Yet the days went by, and Muppim pored over his Hebrew Bible in silence, and kept his sorrow in his own heart.

"I want Huppim to take care of Ard, and to be in the shop this morning," said Naomi, one day. "I have work to do; so, Muppim, you must go alone with Charlie Fay to school."

Huppim did not care to lose his walk, but Naomi knew which of the boys to choose on such an occasion; for Huppim was far more ready to give up his own will and pleasure for others, than was his brother.

Huppim made no great effort about such matters, it is true, but he had a careless, joyous spirit, that made him quite indifferent as to where or how he spent his time. He could be as happy frolicking with Ard, as taking the fresh air with Charlie Fay. As Muppim started off with Charlie, the thought passed through his mind that now he had an opportunity to talk over the subject upon which he had of late so frequently dwelt; but how to begin, he did not know.

Charlie was in excellent spirits. Having become in a measure accustomed to his blindness, his natural joyousness had returned to him, and he almost skipped along, holding fast to Muppim's hand as he went, and talking as cheerfully as in the good old days when they were little children together.

"I say, Muppim, did you know I had found out what was on the card?" said Charlie, giving his companion's arm a suggestive pull. Muppim had been rather absent-minded, and had left Charlie to do the most of the talking.

"Have you?" said Muppim, with sudden interest.

"Yes, I knew the O first, and then the F., and after thinking a while, I guessed it! 'Our Father' came right into my mind, and then of course it was easy to tell all the rest," said Charlie.

"Do you know all the prayer?" asked Muppim.

"Of course I do!" said Charlie, with surprise. "I used to say it when I couldn't speak plain. I didn't know what it meant then, but I love it dearly now."

"I like it, too," said Muppim, quietly.

A thrill of joy passed through Charlie's heart. "And you say it, too, sometimes—you really pray it?" questioned the blind boy. How he wished he could see Muppim's face at that moment!

"I do," was Muppim's only answer.

"It is the prayer our dear Lord Jesus gave to His disciples!" said Charlie, boldly; and as he spoke he inwardly sent up a petition that the Giver of the prayer would bless the words to his young companion.

If Charlie had seen Muppim's face then, he would have been astonished at the strong feeling it displayed.

Now Muppim knew, for the first time, that the prayer which had become a part of his daily devotions, had first come from the lips of that Jesus of whom he had lately thought so much.

Muppim had been taught that the King of the Jews was yet to come, and that Jesus had only pretended to that honor.

Now he felt afraid he had been doing wrong in even speaking words that Jesus had given to His disciples.

Muppim continued silent until they reached the Blind Asylum, and Charlie did not interrupt his meditations. Charlie realized that they had an unseen companion on their walk, with whom he could hold communion without spoken words; and to that companion he prayed most earnestly for Muppim, even as they trod together the busy streets of the city.

When Muppim found himself alone, he gave himself up entirely to his own reflections.

He recalled the conversation he had had with Naomi on the day when he was thirteen. The mother had spoken most solemnly to her sons on the obligations now to rest upon them. She had told them that they were called to serve a holy and just God, to whom they must one day give an account, and had urged upon them to keep the whole law, and to walk in the way of God's commandments.

The thought came home to Muppim's mind with power, that he was living in a Christian country, and had an opportunity to know all of the religion of Jesus;—what excuse then could he give, if that religion were true, and he had not examined it? Muppim was deep in these meditations, when he ran against a stout gentleman, who seemed purposely to put himself in the boy's way.

"So! so! Muppim, what's the matter?" said the friendly voice of Mr. Thayer. "It won't do to be in such a brown study in the public streets. Every body might not take being run over as patiently as I do; though to be sure, I did try to see whether you would turn out for me. Muppim, I was just going to see you."

"To see me!" said Muppim, with surprise.

"Yes," said Mr. Thayer, hesitating slightly. "Now you are learning to read English, I have a book for you, the best book printed in the English language, or any other. I have had it for you some time, but I wanted to look it over first myself, for a reason I had. I have marked some passages that I think will interest you particularly."

"Thank you! thank you! You are very kind," said Muppim, taking the parcel in his hands. It was tied up with a string, and he did not open it as long as Mr. Thayer walked at his side.

The old gentleman soon parted with his young friend, and then Muppim's busy fingers untied the knot.

He started, as he read the title-page, "Holy Bible." Could Mr. Thayer have guessed the thoughts that had lately agitated his mind? Should he read the book? "I will at least compare these

Scriptures with ours," said Muppim to himself; and with this resolution fully formed, Muppim glanced at a Psalm or two, and then returned the book to its wrapper.

"What have you got there?" said Huppim, his observing eyes noting the parcel as soon as Muppim entered the shop.

Muppim did not condescend to reply, but walked straight on to the upper room. Huppim gave a low whistle, which Ard forthwith proceeded to imitate, and Huppim's vexation went off in a laugh at Ard's unsuccessful experiment.

Muppim was by no means the courteous, kindly person he should have been at home. Ard knew when Muppim was in a mood to be let alone, and even Naomi felt at times afraid to intrude upon Muppim's silence.

Huppim often wished in his heart that his brother was more like Charlie Fay, and wondered what made such a difference between them. That evening Muppim seemed in a particularly bad humor. He had not had a moment he could call his own all day, and the book he so longed to examine was still hidden in his drawer, and tied up in its wrapper. There had been errands to do in distant parts of the city, and customers to be waited on in the shop, until Muppim's small store of patience was quite exhausted.

Ard was perched up at the little table in the family room, and was striking two old chair slats together to his great delight.

"Don't, Ard. You make my head ache!" exclaimed Muppim, sharply.

"Bye-bye!" said Ard, folding the two sticks to his bosom, and seeming to hush a baby to sleep.

Huppim laughed, and Muppim said, angrily, "Mother, I wish you would keep the boys still. They make my head ache!"

"One boy is such a little fellow, I think you will have to excuse him," said Naomi, gently. "You had better go to bed, my son, if your head feels so badly."

"I am thirteen!—too old to be sent to bed like a baby!" said Muppim, quickly.

"Not too old to honor your mother," said Naomi, reproachfully.

Muppim lighted a candle and walked up to his own room. He knew that no one would follow him when he was in such a mood, and that he was sure of a few moments of solitude. He opened Mr. Thayer's present. His eyes fell on the few words, "Love as brethren; be pitiful, be courteous."

He turned eagerly to see if they were in the Old Testament, and tried to persuade himself that they did not rebuke him, since they were in the New.

Muppim really loved his mother and his brothers; he did not understand why he had spoken to them so roughly. His head really did ache. It was in vain for him to try to read, the letters swam before his eyes.

He felt dizzy and sick, and would have gladly called some one to help him undress, but he was too proud to ask a favor now of the dear friends from whom he had so rudely parted. Miserable in body and mind, poor Muppim lay down on his bed, but not to sleep.

XIII.

The Sick-Room.

MORNING came with its warm sunlight, and the great city was awake, and all was stir and activity. In Muppim's room there was darkness and stillness. A heavy shawl was hung before the small window to shut out the light that seemed to him to glare so painfully, even through the tiny cracks and crevices left uncovered.

The rattling of the carts on the pavement was cruel torture to his aching head; the very air seemed to burn his brow rather than to cool it.

Naomi sat silently at the bedside. She had never known before what it was to see a child of hers sick and suffering. How she wished that Jacob was at hand to tell what to do! She felt helpless and inexperienced, and full of fear.

There was nothing to reassure Muppim's anxious eyes in her sad, troubled countenance.

He was very ill then, as he suspected; surely, such pains, such sickness could not be common. Muppim trembled at the thought of possible death near at hand.

The physician came, but only to prescribe some remedies, and add his solemn looks to the evidence Muppim already had of his condition.

Then came days of suffering and nights of pain. Naomi's face grew paler and more anxious. Jacob was at hand to lift the sickboy, and to give his help in the long watching in the quiet room.

Huppim by turns tried to keep Ard still, and then joined with him in his romps, stopping with a sudden consciousness that this was no time for play. To Huppim, the world seemed all changed. He missed his brother every hour, and wished he could be allowed to see him now and then, and do something for him instead of standing behind the counter, or trying to keep Ard cool and pleasant.

There was a new face in Naomi's family room, and gentle hands were bathing Muppim's hot forehead, and giving him cooling drinks. Naomi was quite worn out. She could bear up no longer, and Mrs. Fay had insisted upon taking her place, for a few hours at least, that she might have a good quiet rest. That was not the first act of kindness Naomi had experienced from her Christian neighbors, in this time of trial.

Naomi had but few friends of her own nation, none with whom she had been intimate. There was no one who loved her well enough to go to a house where a person was ill with a malignant fever; no one cared to peril life for the sake of the poor sick boy and his weary mother.

Mrs. Fay needed no urging to bring her to Naomi's side. Muppim was dear for his own sake, and Mrs. Fay wanted to be with him, and Charlie would not let her rest at home. He was sure no one could nurse Muppim so gently as his own mother, with her light, loving touch.

Mrs. Fay's foot had been on the stairway, and her hand upon Muppim's door many a time since his illness, and Huppim's spirits had been kept up by many a talk with Charlie Fay.

Mrs. Fay was sitting at Muppim's side when he suddenly opened his eyes, and looked about him in his right mind.

"Mother! where's mother?" said the sick boy, in a faint tone.

Naomi was called, and she bent tenderly down beside her child, while Mrs. Fay quietly withdrew.

"Mother, am I going to die?" said Muppim, looking directly into her face, as he spoke.

Naomi's tears dropped thick and fast, but she made no reply.

"Am I going to die?" repeated Muppim, still more earnestly.

"I hope not!" was all Naomi answered, but her suppressed sobs told how much stronger were her fears than her hopes.

"Can't you comfort me, mother? I am terribly afraid," said Muppim, piteously. Naomi was silent. What did she *know* of the world beyond the grave? God, she was sure, was holy and just; her son had sinned, had broken the fifth Commandment on the very eve of his sickness. "God is just, my son," was the mother's tardy answer.

Muppim groaned and turned away.

He saw himself as he had never seen himself before. "God is just!" Those were words of terror to a selfish, wilful boy, who had openly transgressed, times without number.

"God is just!" the words were fixed in Muppim's mind, like the nail driven home by a strong hand.

With the remembrances of the sins of his youth, there mingled a new feature of terror. The vision of a crucified one hanging in agony on a cross, was before his eyes. This Jesus, this sufferer *might* be the true Messiah,—then what would be the punishment of the Jew who had only spoken his name in scorn!

Muppim lay long in bitter, anxious thought. At length he said, "Mother, I want to see Charlie Fay."

Charlie needed no second invitation to call him to his sick friend. "Dear Charlie," said Muppim, who felt in that hour of trial how precious his blind friend was to his heart.

Charlie kissed the sufferer, and said cheerfully, "I am so glad to be near you once more, Muppim!"

"You won't have me long," said Muppim, bitterly. "I am going to die! I am horribly afraid, Charlie; can you comfort me?"

"Why are you afraid, Muppim?" said Charlie, tenderly.

"God is just!" groaned the poor boy, in his distress.

"Yes, we all deserve punishment, but because Jesus suffered for us, God will forgive us and make us happy forever, if we are sorry for our sins and trust in Christ Jesus."

"But I have not trusted in him; I have hated to hear his name," said Muppim, despairingly.

"He will forgive you gladly. He prayed for the very men who nailed him to the cross, 'Father, forgive them, they know not what they do!' You are not worse than they were. You have not known what you were doing."

"But I might have known," urged Muppim.

"Jesus will forgive you; now, will you let me ask him?"

"I do not know as it is right," said poor Muppim, and even as he spoke, his mind wandered, and he began to talk of the birds that were fluttering about him, and to try to catch them with his thin weak fingers.

Muppim's short season of consciousness was over; again he was but speaking wildly, as one in a dream.

Charlie did not give up seeking the forgiveness of Jesus for his friend, though that friend could not join in his prayer.

To him who forgave the Jews of old, Charlie prayed for the young son of Israel, who in his extremity had turned like the thief on the cross, to Jesus as his only hope. That ignorant, dying thief was forgiven, and Charlie was not in despair.

Muppim might yet see in the New Jerusalem the Saviour, whom he had never known on earth.

XIV.

Good News.

ARD was sitting on the floor in the family room, busy with trying to make a teacup stand on an empty spool.

Huppim came suddenly down the stairway and snatched up the child, and bore him triumphantly into the shop in spite of his struggles and laughing exclamations.

"There, now!" said Huppim, setting the little fellow down on the counter. "There, that is because Muppim is better, and we are going to have good times again. Aren't you glad, Ard? say, now!"

Ard clapped his hands and gave vent to his joy by a regular cock-crow, and as good a "moo—" as could be expected of a child who had seen so little of cows.

"Take Ard, mother, or he'll fall off!" said Huppim to Naomi, who came in at the moment. "Take him. I want to go tell the news to Charlie Fay."

"Muppim is not safe yet," said Naomi, anxiously.

"But he's better, and Charlie ought to know it!" said Huppim, darting away with a beaming face.

It would have been hard indeed long to keep from Charlie a piece of intelligence which gave him so much pleasure. He had a double joy in Muppim's recovery. His playfellow was to be restored to him, and restored to him, he believed, to be a true Christian.

While Muppim had lain upon his sick-bed, trembling between life and death, Charlie had prayed long and frequently for him. The blind boy, moreover, had been preparing himself to guide his dear friend, if his life should be spared, into the knowledge of Jesus. He had heard his mother read over the prophecies respecting our Saviour, and then the passages in the New Testament which record the fulfilment of these prophecies. Charlie had always been a good scholar at school, but now he bent his whole mind to the task he had laid out for himself, and learned with wonderful ease and rapidity. He wanted to have his mind stored with the treasures of the Scriptures, that he might unfold them to Muppim, whenever a fit opportunity should come.

The news that Muppim was really better redoubled Charlie's interest in his studies, and he was soon able to repeat chapter after chapter of the New Testament without hesitation. The labor he had undertaken for the sake of his friend made his time pass away very pleasantly, and precious to dwell upon were the words of the Holy Book which he had thus stored away in his mind.

The time came at last when Muppim could sit, bolstered up in Mrs. Fay's great chintz-covered easy-chair, which she had lent to Naomi for the purpose. Very tall and slender Muppim looked, leaning back there in his dressing-gown. His face was thin and dark, and his black eyes had a sorrowful, anxious expression, piteous to behold. His troubled countenance was but the reflection of his troubled heart.

Muppim was truly grateful that he had not been called into the presence of his Maker, but his mind was all in wild confusion about religious things. He longed to have a quiet talk with Charlie; but his head felt too weak, his voice was too feeble for him to speak out the thoughts that vexed him day and night. Meanwhile Muppim had framed silent prayers of his own to the crucified. "O Jesus!" he would say in his heart, "if thou art the king of the Jews, forgive me all that is past; and if thou art not, O God, forgive me and guide me into the knowledge of the truth."

The days went by, and Muppim slowly gained his strength, but summer was fading into autumn before he began to look at all like his former self. By degrees his room had ceased to be actually a sick-room, and had grown a place of family gathering. Ard might now be heard coming up stairs, and stopping as he mounted each step, to give a little chuckle to congratulate himself on the achievement. He even dared to drag about Muppim's room the old shoe which served him for a carriage, and in which newspaper doll-babies rode as contentedly as in a gilded coach.

Naomi sat but seldom now in the lower

room, which was her old resort; her place seemed fixed at Muppim's low window, and there she was to be seen whenever her presence was not required below.

Naomi was thin and pale with much watching, but there was a joyous sweetness on her face, as she saw her dear boy gaining from day to day. Cheerfully, encouragingly she talked to him, and wondered at his anxious, serious look. She wished Huppim could be more up stairs and give out some of his life there. Huppim was quite the shop-keeper in these days. Jacob was almost constantly in the country making up for the time he had lost in the sick-room, and Huppim thought himself particularly entrusted with the business matters of the family, during his father's absence. Indeed, he did show an uncommon talent for accounts, and could make a dime into a dollar as easily by trading as any boy in the city.

His father saw this tendency with an approving eye, and thought one of his sons at least was coming on well in the path he had marked out for him. It is not to be supposed that Huppim was never in his brother's room. He made flying trips there to tell of funny occurrences that had taken place in the shop, and to win a passing smile from Muppim, but the truth must be told, Huppim was of too lively a nature to care to be pent up long between four walls, with nothing outward to vary his thoughts.

It was on Charlie Fay that Muppim relied for companionship. Charlie had once been as fond of fun and the open air as Huppim himself, but he had learned another lesson now, and it was a privilege to him to sit beside his friend, and talk in his own cheerful way until Muppim's tones grew less sad, and an occasional laugh was heard from him.

Charlie well knew that Muppin was not in a condition to have agitating subjects brought before his mind. He waited patiently for the time to come when Muppim would feel himself strong enough to enter upon the topic that he was sure was never far from his thoughts. One pleasant day in September, Charlie was sitting alone with Muppim, when the young Jew suddenly asked, "What did you sing, Charlie, on the morning of the Passover?"

"I don't know: was it this?"—

Charlie sang the whole of the hymn beginning,

> "Guide me, O thou great Jehovah,
>   Pilgrim through this barren land,
> I am weak, but thou art mighty,
>   Hold me with thy powerful hand."

Muppin listened with interest, then said, "No, not that, but that is very beautiful."

"Yes, that is one of my favorites. Oh, I remember, I had been thinking of Jesus, the true Lamb of the Passover, shedding his blood for us. I sang,

> "Come, let us sing of Jesus,
>   The sinner's only friend,
> Come, let us sing of Jesus,
>   While hearts and accents blend."

"That was it! that was it!" said Muppim, very earnestly. "That set me to thinking. I don't feel about Jesus as I did, Charlie, but I am troubled about him. I don't understand"—

Muppim put his hand to his head.

"You are weak," said Charlie, tenderly. "He does not want you to think too deeply now; let me just tell you some of his own precious words. 'Let not your heart be troubled: ye believe in God, believe also in me. If a man love me, he will keep my words: and my Father will love him, and we will come unto him, and make our abode with him. These things have I spoken unto you, being yet present with you. But the Comforter, which is the Holy Ghost, whom the Father will send in my name, he shall teach you all things, and bring all things to your remembrance, whatsoever I have said unto you. Peace I leave with you, my peace I give unto you, not as the world giveth, give I unto you. Let not your heart be troubled, neither let it be afraid.'"

"Let not your heart be troubled, neither let it be afraid!" These were, indeed, precious words to Muppim, and they sank into his heart like a message of peace. He was ready to be guided into the truth, and he would wait to be led in God's good time, when his poor weak head could study and think once more.

Muppim was beginning to understand something of the gentleness and mercy of God in Christ Jesus.

XV.

A Young Disciple.

NAOMI was a true mother, and she watched her son with the interest that only a mother can feel. She saw that he was still thoughtful and subdued, but the wild, anxious look had gone from his eye, and she rejoiced at the change. She little knew how often he repeated to himself, "Let not your heart be troubled, ye believe in God, believe also in me."

Little by little Charlie Fay had recited to Muppim much of the beautiful teaching of our Saviour, giving with it the saying of that Saviour, "My doctrine is not mine, but his that sent me. If any man will do his will, he shall know of the doctrine, whether it be of God, or whether I speak of myself."

Muppim had it set before him what it was to be lovely and gentle, meek, humble, and forgiving. He saw the beauty of holiness, as taught by the Lord Jesus, and felt his own unworthiness.

He was too weak now to argue and reason, but he could try to follow this holy teaching, and take home the kind command, " Let not your heart be troubled."

Ard now dared to pluck his brother's sleeve, and call his attention to his tower of chips, or his faithful horse the rocking-chair, which could move so much and get on so little. Huppim did not find Muppim in moods when he could not be approached, and Naomi somehow felt that her dear son was more such as she wished, than he had ever been before.

Muppim had a daily pleasure now, through the kindness of Mr. Thayer, who had not forgotten his little friend in the time of his sickness. Flowers, and cooling drinks, fruit, and nice, nourishing food, he had sent him from time to time, and now in the bright dry weather, a carriage drew up every day before Jacob Myers' shop, for Muppim to take a long drive, far, far beyond the city's utmost bounds.

Charlie Fay was always one of the party in the carriage, and sometimes Huppim was there with his lively chat, or Naomi, holding the delighted, prattling Ard upon her knee.

So with careful nursing, pleasant company, and good fresh air, the young Jew was gently led back to the strength of health.

When Muppim no longer felt the strange dizziness in his head, that had so troubled him, he began upon the study for which he had so longed, even the faithful study of the Scriptures of the Old and New Testament. Mr. Thayer's gift was taken from its wrapper, to become Muppim's constant companion. It was plain that other eyes had carefully read that book before. Along the margin there were pencil-marks, wherever there was a prophecy of the Messiah, and a reference made to the New Testament passage in which this prophecy was fulfilled.

Muppim read of a promised Saviour who should destroy the works of the devil, and while he ruled his people, suffer for their sins. He read of one who should meekly bear persecution and reproach, and should yet be the King of the Jews, the son of David, "the mighty God," born at Bethlehem, the child of a virgin, of the family of David,—a Deliverer was to come who would lead forth his people like a shepherd, and gather all nations unto him. He was to suffer as no man had yet suffered, and to reign as no man had yet reigned.

So spake the Old Testament* to Muppim. In the New, he read of Christ coming in the appointed way, walking in perfect holiness, casting out devils by his own power, fulfilling the prophecies, even to the casting of lots for his garments, and the drinking of vinegar on the cross. He, the Only Begotten Son of God, was pleased to suffer for our sins, and call both Jews and Gentiles to wash away their guilt in his most precious blood.

This surely was the Lamb, of which all other sacrifices were but types and signs. This Jesus must be the true Messiah.

It had been foretold that the sacrifices should cease at Jerusalem when Messiah appeared.† After Christ's death the Jews were scattered abroad, their temple was

---

* See "The Lock and the Key," (published by the American Tract Society,) a comparison of the Old Testament prophecies of Christ, with their recorded fulfilment in the New Testament.

†Daniel ix, 26, 27.

destroyed, and even at the Passover, the lamb was no longer slain.

There was no need of the death of animals as a sign that blood must be shed for sin, now that Jesus had come to suffer for the sins of the whole world.

Day after day the young Jew read, prayed, and pondered. Ah! would that many of his dear nation would do likewise.

Jesus, in his loveliness, and his wonderful mercy, was slowly revealed to Muppim's eager search.

Adoring, he at length cast himself on his knees, exclaiming like Thomas, "My Lord and my God!"

Muppim had become in heart a Christian Jew. A Jew he must ever be, by nation; he would not have renounced that privilege. He was of the same people as Moses and the prophets. The Virgin Mary and the twelve disciples were of that people to which the blessed Saviour, as a man, had chosen to belong. Over that nation the Saviour has promised again to reign, and in their prosperity the Gentiles shall rejoice. Even heaven is known as the New Jerusalem, and he who wept over the ancient city of his love, will be himself the light of the new city that shall be called by the name so dear to every child of Israel.

Muppim was more heartily a Jew than ever before, yet most sincerely a Christian. His head owned that the prophecies were fulfilled in Christ, the Messiah; his heart trusted and loved Jesus, the Saviour, the merciful, all-sufficient Redeemer. The peace which Jesus has promised to his true followers settled upon Muppim's soul, peace and joy made glad his countenance.

XVI.

Bravo.

MUPPIM was in his own room, busy with his favorite book. "Come! come down, Muppim," said the voice of his brother, from the foot of the stairs.

A look of impatience at the interruption passed over Muppim's face, followed by an expression of shame, and an inward prayer for forgiveness. This seeking of his own pleasure was not like the unselfish spirit of Jews, which Muppim was trying to practise.

In a moment his voice answered, cheerfully, "Yes, Huppim, I am coming."

That unusual effort was not unnoticed by the observing Huppim, and he wondered what new motive was latterly leading

Muppim to trample on his natural faults, and to do the things most trying to him.

"Come on," said Huppim, slipping his arm into that of his brother, as soon as he appeared, "come and see Charlie Fay's present from Mr. Thayer."

Anything concerning Charlie was always interesting to Muppim, and he went on without delay.

Charlie was kneeling on the floor of his room, caressing a splendid dog, that put his head lovingly against the boy, as if already understanding that he was to be his master.

"Why!" exclaimed Muppim, "it is the Blind Asylum dog. It is Bravo! Is he to be yours, Charlie?"

"Mr. Thayer bought him and gave him to me, and the good fellow seems to understand it. See how he puts his head against me and licks my hand! He has always seemed fond of me. Isn't it delightful? I should not be afraid to go any where with Bravo. See, when I put my hand in his collar, he won't let me hit the chairs, put them where you will, about the room."

The boys put the room into utter confusion, and then Charlie got up to cross it, holding on to Bravo's collar.

The sagacious dog gently led the blind boy about, avoiding any obstacle, and keeping his eye upon him, as a tender mother would upon her tottering, lisping little one.

"Now that is a present worth having!" said Huppim, heartily.

"Isn't it!" was Charlie's enthusiastic response.

Muppim admired the dog, too, but he more warmly and deeply felt the beautiful spirit of his friend, who was so truly grateful to be led by a dumb animal, rather than repining, because the use of his own eyes was denied him.

This surely was the work of the Holy Spirit, given by the Lord Jesus, to his true followers!

"How Ard would like to see Bravo!" said Huppim. "I must go home and tell him about him!"

Away went the restless Huppim, while Charlie threw his arm round the patient dog, who sat down at his side; Muppim sat down too. He had much to say to Charlie, and might not soon have another private opportunity.

"Charlie," said Muppim, "dear Charlie, I am quite happy now; I have found him of whom Moses and the prophets did write. I believe he is my Saviour. Oh, how I thank you! It was your patience in your trial that made me first think there must be truth in the religion of Jesus!"

Charlie put his head upon his hands, and tears trickled from his sightless eyes.

"O God, I thank thee!" he murmured. "O God, I thank thee! This is joy that more than exceeds all my sorrow!"

"Muppim," he added, after a pause, "Muppim, I am glad I am blind, if so you have learned to see your Saviour!"

"Dear Charlie!" said the young Jew, not less affected, "Dear Charlie, God will reward you; I can do nothing for you, but try to follow your example. But, Charlie, I find myself so full of faults! Only just now I felt cross to leave my books when Huppim called me."

"We ought certainly to be willing to struggle to do right for Jesus' sake, when he has done so much for us," said Charlie. "Mother read to me only this morning the parable of the sower, and I noticed that they only are like the good seed on good ground, who *bear fruit with* PATIENCE. It is so natural to want to be good all at once, instead of being willing to let God work slowly in us as it pleases him best. I am afraid I have been very impatient about you, Muppim. I wanted you to see the truth at once; I could hardly wait for your slow studying out what seemed to me so plain!"

"I *felt* it all true long ago," said Muppim, "but it is only lately that I could really see the proofs, and feel, oh! so certain!"

"What does your mother say, Muppim?" asked Charlie, with much interest.

Muppim's brow suddenly clouded.— "Mother, poor mother! I have not said a word to her yet. I cannot bear to grieve her so."

"Perhaps she may follow where you have led. You ought to be frank with her at once, Muppim," was the quick answer.

"I know it! Of course she must hear

all. Every Jew in town will hear it, and they will hate and despise me!" said Muppim, bitterly.

"'The disciple is not better than his Master.' The Jews cried out, Crucify him!'" said Charlie, quietly.

"I know it. I am ready to bear all for his sake," said Muppim, with much earnestness, "but I cannot bear to distress my mother. Huppim too! I do not believe he will speak to me—and my father, he will be ready to kill me! Oh, Charlie, you do not know how to be grateful for your Christian mother."

"I know how to love her! But indeed, I feel, Muppim, that you have trials of which I know nothing. Mine has been a very happy lot," said Charlie.

Muppim looked at the sightless eyes of his grateful friend, and was rebuked; should not he too receive meekly whatever trials it pleased his Heavenly Father to send? He would at once boldly avow his belief in the Lord Jesus, and take the consequences in meek submission. Muppim declared his determination, and then the two friends knelt for such true prayer as God loves to hear.

XVII.

The Announcement.

NAOMI was sitting in the inner room at her work, when Muppim entered, fresh from his prayer with Charlie Fay.

Huppim, busy with a customer, saw his brother pass through the shop, and wondered at the paleness of his face and the deep earnestness of his expression.

"Mother, I want to see you alone," said Muppim, solemnly.

"What is the matter, my son? Have you bad news to tell? Your father—has anything happened to him?" asked Naomi, laying her hand beseechingly on Muppim's shoulder.

"I have news of which the angels are

glad," said Muppim, as he led the way to the upper room.

"Not now, dear," said Muppim, gently but decidedly, as Ard pressed on to follow his mother.

"Go to Huppim, dear; go," and Muppim put his own cap on the little fellow's head, who trotted away to the shop, to show himself thus ornamented.

Naomi sat down on the side of the low bed, and looked eagerly at Muppim as he closed the door.

"Mother," said Muppim, earnestly, "do you remember how you talked with me in this very room, on the day I was thirteen? Do you remember how you told me that I now stood before the Great God to answer for my own sins, and to keep the law, as a true Jew?"

"I remember," replied Naomi, faintly; "what wicked thing have you done, my son?"

"I felt what you said, mother, and I have sought with all my heart to know my duty; I have tried to do it, and I believe God has watched over me and led me right."

Naomi kissed her boy in grateful joy, and then again the troubled expression came over her face as she said, "What is it then that you have to tell me? Speak out, Muppim," and the mother's fears were again uppermost.

"It is of myself I want to speak, mother," said Muppim. "Mother, I have studied our Hebrew Scriptures, I have prayed much to the God of our fathers, I have read all that is told of the true Messiah, and I have found him—I have found the Promised One; I know him and he knows me."

A wild thought for a moment passed through Naomi's mind: Perhaps her dear son had been honored to be the "prophet," the "Elias," who was to come before the Messiah, and tell of him! This was a moment of exaltation and joy, but it was followed by one of bitter abasement, as her son exclaimed, "Jesus is my Saviour! He, mother, is the Christ! To him I trust my soul! I am a Christian!"

Naomi's usual gentleness forsook her: in sudden anger she thrust her son from her, exclaiming, "I despise you! I cast you off!"

Muppim closed his eyes and stood in silent prayer. In another instant, his mother's arms were thrown round him, and she wept bitter tears as she exclaimed, "Oh, my son! my poor son!"

It was vain for Muppim to strive to tell of the new joy and peace he had found in Christ Jesus. His mother laid her hand upon his mouth, and would not permit him to speak such words in her presence. She poured forth her distress in one stream of tender reproaches, to which Muppim listened with pity, praying the while, that she whom he loved best might one day know that Christ, for whose sake he was willing to be despised and reviled.

Even while Naomi was speaking, she wondered to see Muppim, who had once been so impatient of the slightest rebuke, meeting her eye with an expression of love and patience that could not be mistaken.

Having exhausted her arguments and reproofs, Naomi said, " Muppim, you cannot be allowed to be with the other children, lest you should lead them into your terrible error; here you must stay until your father comes home, and he can best decide what is to be done with you. My poor child! this will go far to break your father entirely—he had hoped so much from you." Naomi's tears overcame her, and she sat down again.

"Dear, dear mother, I am so sorry to grieve you," said Muppim, tenderly.

Naomi leaned her head upon the shoulder of her tall boy, and wept for a few moments in silence.

"Perhaps you may one day see the truth as I do, and then we might be happy together! Dear mother, do search the Scriptures, and know more of Jesus," Muppim ventured to say.

Naomi's tears were suddenly dried; jumping up quickly, she went out, locking the door behind her.

Muppim was left to solitary confinement, but he did not feel himself alone. Grieved as he was to have so pained his mother, he rejoiced that he was counted worthy to suffer for such a Lord. That Lord he felt was with him, a better comforter than any earthly friend.

Muppim had been praying most earnestly for his own dear family, when he heard

Ard's uncertain footsteps on the stairs. The brother's heart went out towards the child, and he longed to admit him, and talk to him of the Saviour, who said, "Suffer the little children to come unto me."

Poor Muppim was obliged to have quite a different kind of intercourse with the pet of the house. Ard knocked violently at the door, to assure himself that Muppim was within. No sooner had Muppim replied, "Brother can't let you in, darling," than Ard burst forth, "Bad boy! Old, bad boy! Ard strike bad boy!"

The little fist came hard against the door again and again, and words even more harsh and contemptuous came from the lips of the child, as he strove to show by every outward demonstration his horror of his brother.

Muppim was not affectionate in his

manner, but he was strong in his attachments; he had hardly realized how dear Ard was to him, until he felt the bitterness of being reproached and reviled by those young lips, and despised by that young heart. The tears actually came in Muppim's eyes; but he remembered his Lord and Master, forsaken even by his disciples, and resolved to take his smaller trials cheerfully.

"Dear little brother," Muppim found voice to say, "Dear Ard, Muppim loves you very dearly, and would like to give you one kiss just now."

"Ain't you cross in there? Ain't you mad at me?" said Ard, in surprise, applying his eye at the same time to the key-hole.

"I am not angry at you, darling. Brother Muppim means never to get angry again."

"I see you; you look real pleasant,"

said the little fellow. "I wish I could get in."

"Ard! Ard!" called the mother's voice from below, and again the uncertain footsteps were heard on the stairs, the lower door closed, and Muppim was left to his meditations.

XVIII.

The Prisoner.

MUPPIM had been two days in solitary confinement, save when Naomi had come to plead with him to give up his delusion, and be once more her own dear son. She even pledged herself to keep his avowal to her a secret, if he would but once more be heartily a Jew, and forget what had passed. At each interview, her face grew more sad and stern. Muppim's fare was reduced to a scanty supply of bread and water, which Naomi declared was quite too good for one like him.

Muppim had no human being to speak with, but he was not without sympathy. He could hear Charlie Fay singing his favorite hymns in the next house, and now and then Charlie's flute would sound out its sweet, sad tones. The blind boy had developed a wonderful talent for music, and Mr. Thayer was giving him every opportunity of improving it. The cheerful sounds from Charlie's room were a continual lesson to Muppim, and he resolved, like a caged bird, to give forth only a grateful song in his own confinement. At midnight on the third day of Muppim's disgrace, he was roused from sleep by a hand's being laid upon his shoulder. He looked up, and Huppim stood by the bedside with a shaded candle in his hand.

"Huppim! how came you here?" said Muppim, starting up in bed.

"Hush!" said the visitor, putting his fingers to his lips. "Hush! I got the key out of mother's pocket, while she was asleep. I would come to see you. I have brought you some cold meat, and a piece of pie. You must be terribly hungry."

Muppim looked wistfully at the food, but said, decidedly, "I do not like to take it, Huppim. You are very, very kind; but mother said I must eat nothing but bread and water. I am sorry to grieve her. I at least can obey her."

"What a queer boy you are!" said Huppim, half provoked. "I took so much pains to get to you!"

"And I am very glad to see you," said Muppim, more affectionately than he had ever spoken before. "I never loved any of you half as well as I do now."

"You don't seem like yourself, Muppim. You are so gentle and quiet. Why, if I were you, I should be just as mad as I could be, to be shut up here. I wouldn't stay —I wouldn't. I'd just jump out of the window and be off. I don't see what it is all about. I can't understand how a Jew can be anything else than a Jew. If being a Christian was being like Charlie Fay,

I shouldn't mind it myself, but I can't see how that can be; we are not the same kind of folks."

"I am just as much a Jew as ever," said Muppim, "and glad to be of the same race as Messiah. But, Huppim, I do believe in the Lord Jesus as the Christ, and love him with all my heart, and I wish you did, too."

"I am more like father; I don't take hold of these things, somehow, as you do," replied Huppim, thoughtfully.

"But, dear brother, you have got to die all alone, just as I have, and then when Jesus sits on the throne to judge the world, you will have to answer for it, if you have never tried to know him. Won't you think of that, Huppim? The Jews are looking for the Messiah, and will not see that he has already come."

"I never thought much about him, any way," said Huppim. "But what are you going to do, shut up here? When father comes home, he will whip the skin off from you, just as likely as not. I'd run away before, if I were in your place. I don't know what's to become of me. Mother don't let me speak to Charlie Fay, and he don't know what's the matter. I'm sure he thinks it hard of me. If it wasn't for Bravo, he wouldn't get to school at all. I tell you, Muppim, that's a great dog! He'll fetch and carry. He knows almost as much as a boy!"

"He must be a real comfort to Charlie. I am so glad he has him," said Muppim, warmly.

"Now, Muppim, you are queer. You seem just as pleasant as ever. It is real good to see you; but I must be off, or mother 'll find out. I wouldn't have her know I'd been in here for a pretty penny."

"Dear Huppim, it has been a real treat to see you; but don't come again secretly.

It is not right to do it without mother's leave. It is very pleasant to me to know that you don't feel hard towards me."

"Not a bit of it!" said Huppim, warmly. "I never liked you half so well in my life. Somehow that sickness did you a heap of good! You seem like a different boy, totally."

"If there is anything good in me, Huppim, it is because the Lord Jesus, whom I am trying to serve, helps me, and is ever with me. If you only knew him as I do, I should be very, very happy!"

"Well, you certainly tell well for your new way of thinking," said Huppim. "I wouldn't mind being somewhat improved myself. But I must say good-night to you. I sha'n't promise not to come to see you again. I like the fun. As the key is on my side now, I can do as I please. Time was, when you used to lock me out," said Muppim, mischievously.

"I was selfish often, I know. I see it quite plainly now, and I want you to forgive me for not being a better brother to you; will you?" asked Muppim, earnestly.

"Why, Muppim! You hate to own up to anything, and *you* say that! Of course we are quits. I have nothing laid up against you. Why, old fellow! what's got into you?" For the first time since babyhood, the brothers kissed affectionately, and so they parted.

XIX.

Discipline.

JACOB MYERS was thoroughly angry, when on his return he found out what had occurred during his absence. Jacob thought it no sin to have all his thoughts and all his interest in his worldly business. He thought it no sin to talk of his bargains in the synagogue between the prayers, or even while he had the holy words on his lips, to be adding up, mentally, dollars and cents. Like too many who call themselves Christians, he was contented with an outside religion for himself and his children, but clung to that as if it were the one thing needful. That one of his family should become a follower of Christ, he thought a disgrace too bitter to be borne, and he resolved to keep the whole matter a secret, and try and bring back his boy to his own way of thinking.

Jacob was not much of a scholar, and he had no skill in arguing. He did not undertake to convince Muppim that he had made a mistake; his plan was quite different.

Jacob knew how to use as hard language as any man in the city, and he gave Muppim the benefit of some of the harshest scolding that human lips ever uttered,—not to speak of the outward signs of contempt, so marked among the Jews, to which even our Saviour himself was subjected.

Jacob had, moreover, a certain strong leather whip, which he called his "family regulator," and which was now brought out to do duty.

When Naomi heard the lashes fall thick and fast, with no sound of resistance from

Muppim—not even a scream—her mother's heart felt for him. Again and again Jacob tried the virtue of whipping and scolding, and met only a firm refusal to give up the religion of Jesus, and a meek submission to the punishments imposed.

Jacob's resolution was at length taken. He could not have one black sheep to infect his whole flock. He would not have it known that a son of his had departed from the faith of his fathers, and made himself an object of scorn and hatred to his own people. Muppim should be sent from his home, and not live where he would disgrace his family.

Naomi pleaded for her son, and felt how dear Muppim was to her even now, in his patient endurance of rebuke and chastisement.

Jacob was not to be shaken in his determination. With his own hands he put up Muppim's small wardrobe in a travelling bag, and then told the astonished boy that he was to leave his father's house forever, and go to earn his bread in a distant city, as best he could.

"I wont be hard on you," said Jacob; "you shall have twenty dollars to start with, Muppim. Many a rich man has had less; but never let me see your face again, to my dying day."

Jacob would allow no leave-takings. Naomi was not permitted to say one word to her child. She heard his footsteps as his father led him away. The door closed, and she knew that Muppim was gone from her forever. Then her grief burst forth, and she would not be comforted; indeed, she had no comforter.

Ard had been for some days in a state of rebellion about Muppim's confinement. He declared that his brother was a good boy, and "spoke pleasant," and he should be let out. As for Huppim, his indignation knew no bounds. He said he did not want to be a Jew if Jews could beat and scold a boy like Muppim, just for having his own notions, and he did not care how soon he was turned out too.

Jacob Myers did not return to a happy home that day. The dinner might as well not have been placed on the table, for nobody touched it but Ard, and he ate and sulked, and sulked and ate, in the worst possible humor.

As for Jacob, he felt quite ashamed of himself, now that it was all over;—not ashamed of his harshness, but that his heart so yearned for the absent Muppim.

XX.

Muppim.

JACOB had paid Muppim's fare, and put him in the cars for a distant western city, laying his commands upon him to make no nearer station his stopping-place. Jacob knew that he could depend upon Muppim's implicit obedience. He was but the more faithful keeper of the moral law, for his new principles; that the father well knew.

Muppim could hardly realize that he was alone in the world, as the swift cars bore him rapidly away from his native city. He looked round upon the faces gathered in that long, narrow car. On every countenance there were lines of care and sin. Few there were that bore the traces of being loving or lovable. This was a specimen of the people of this world,—of those for whom Christ died. For such as these he came to suffer the cruel death upon the cross.

More wonderful than ever seemed to Muppim the redeeming love of the Saviour;—that Saviour he knew was then present at his side, and would never leave him desolate.

Muppim took out his dear Bible, and was soon lost to outward circumstances in his interest in it. Mile after mile was passed over, and the young Jew had not raised his head. At length expressions of admiration from the surrounding travellers attracted his attention. His book was laid aside. He was to read no more that day.

Muppim had never been ten miles beyond the bounds of his native city. Rivers shining in the sun, and mountains towering towards the skies, were new sights to him—new evidences of the power and love of the Creator. There were many to speak of the beauty of the changing landscape, but few who looked forth from the swift-moving cars, to praise the Lord for his wonderful works, as did the young Jew on his first journey.

Night came at last, and the scattered villages could only be traced by the twinkling lamps in their quiet homes. One by one those lights went out, and only the ever-shining stars remained to vary the darkness which covered earth and heaven.

Muppim commended himself anew to the care of his Saviour, and then putting his head upon his arm, he fell into as sweet a sleep as Ard was then enjoying in his distant home.

There was a stir and bustle in the cars in the early morning. It was plain that some important stopping-place had been reached. Yes, the city to which Muppim was banished was near at hand. In a few moments Muppim would have to seek some other resting-place than the cars, where he had been so tranquil.

There were eager faces, watching to welcome the passengers as they stepped on the platform. There were mothers, ready to kiss returning school-boys. There were men of business, to take the well-known travellers by the button, and employ the few moments of delay in important conversation. Everybody seemed in a hurry, everybody seemed to know where to go, and what to do.

Muppim felt confused and lonely in the midst of that bustling scene. He strengthened himself with the thought that there was one Being near him, to whom he was not a stranger; One who could guide his footsteps even in that great city.

Muppim took breakfast at the railroad

station, and then, with his small carpet-bag in his hand, he followed the throng pouring towards the main street of the city. There Muppim had resolved to seek a position as clerk. For the small trading of his youth he had no taste. He did not care to make money; he simply wished to earn an honest living, and to have a shelter in some Christian home. We will not tell all the adventures of that weary day. We need not describe the various ways in which Muppim was repulsed and refused. A lad with a Jewish face, and without recommendation or references, was not likely to get a situation at once.

Muppim would not be disheartened. When he went to a third-rate hotel at evening, it was not to give himself up to sorrowful meditations. No! he had quite another plan in his mind. His father had forbidden him to write to any of the family, and had assured him that if he attempted it, his letters would be burnt, unopened. "The Christians may take care of you. You belong to them, now," Jacob had roughly said.

To a certain young Christian, very dear to Muppim, he now resolved to write. Charlie Fay could tell him all about Jacob's home; and in this way, though so far distant, Muppim hoped to hear constant news of his own family, not to speak of the pleasure of holding communication with Charlie, himself. Muppim was sure that Mrs. Fay would willingly act as amanuensis for her unfortunate son, and already he began to enjoy in imagination the agreeable variety of letters from Charlie.

Muppim did not say one word of the trying scenes that had preceded his banishment. He simply stated that his father had sent him from home to make his own way in the world, and had forbidden him to hold any communication with his own family, and therefore any news that Charlie could give of his neighbors would be most acceptable.

Muppim gave no dreary account of his discouraging day. He spoke of the deep satisfaction he had taken in the wonders of nature he had seen on his journey, and of the peace at his heart, assured as he was that Christ would never leave him nor forsake him. When Muppim folded his letter, he could hardly believe that he was in the midst of strangers. Charlie Fay seemed close at hand, and he realized that the Saviour, so dear to them both, was about their path to comfort and cheer.

Three or four days of discouraging applications passed away with Muppim. His little fund was of course diminishing, and he began to think of the possibility of actually coming to want. He had never known what it is to lack the comforts of life, and latterly, since his father's prosperity had increased, he had been supplied with many luxuries.

Muppim trusted in the care of Providence, but he knew that it became him to be prudent and earnest in seeking employment. Before commencing, therefore, upon his fifth day of effort, he changed his boarding-place to a still less attractive and less expensive hotel, where the company was by no means to his taste.

Sallying out to enter new warehouses, and have interviews with more strangers, Muppim renewed his search for a situation. His application had been refused so many times, that he felt that he now spoke as if he expected to be rejected, and had none of the confident, self-respectful air that promotes success. With the heads of the establishments, he could find no fault. They dismissed him shortly, but with no unnecessary harshness. With the clerks it was quite different.

"We are honest here—we don't *Jew*," said one spruce lad behind the counter, in answer to Muppim's inquiry whether there was a vacant position in the store for a clerk. "We keep a sharp look-out for strangers whom nobody knows," said another. These, and other similar attempts at witticisms, were particularly painful to a spirit like Muppim's; but he struggled to bear them with patience, remembering him "who humbled himself to the form of a servant," for our sakes. This day passed away as the others had done. Muppim's future was still uncertain, yet he did not despair. His "daily bread was sure;" though the way of earning it was yet unknown.

Muppim had been for some days on the look-out for an answer from Charlie Fay. Here, too, he had been several times disappointed. A letter for Muppim Myers was waiting for him, however, on the evening of the last and most trying day.

Mrs. Fay could hardly write fast enough to express the loving, Christian sympathy that poured from Charlie's lips. He honored Muppim's silence about his home difficulties, but could easily guess them all. If Charlie had had only sympathy to express, he could have dispatched at once enough of that—but he could not content himself in that way.

Charlie well knew that Jacob Myers would not send forth his son to live in idleness in that western city. But how was Muppim, a stranger, to get employment? This thought Charlie turned over and over in his mind. Muppim's silence on the subject convinced him that the first few days' efforts had been by no means successful. Charlie's meditations ended in taking Bravo by the collar and going out for a long walk, a walk that ended at Mr. Thayer's comfortable home.

Charlie had not mistaken the warm-hearted old gentleman. His interest was at once aroused for Muppim. The boy who had so courageously risked all for Christ, should not be deserted by his Christian friends!

Mr. Thayer well knew that his name had reached the western cities, and was as well known "on change" as if he were the head of a banking institution. In real business style he dashed off short notes to several of the leading merchants in Muppim's present stopping-place. Notes they were of thorough recommendation, to a certain Christian Jew, Muppim Myers, who would be glad of any situation where he could earn an honest living, and who well deserved confidence and kind consideration.

Muppim was astonished when those three

notes dropped from the envelope, containing Charlie's warm-hearted response to his words of inquiry. Charlie had no news to tell of his neighbors, excepting that they were all well, but that nobody about the house seemed cheerful. Even Ard was reported as unusually cross, and Huppim had not been seen with a smile on his face. Of course Charlie had had no direct intercourse with the family, but he and his mother would gladly communicate even the most trifling particulars of their daily life that came under their knowledge.

Charlie had much to say of his love to his distant friend, but not a word of the efforts he had made for him. Mr. Thayer's notes were enclosed with one from himself, telling Muppim to keep up heart, for the best situations were not the easiest to get,—and assuring him that Christ and his Christian friends would not forsake him.

Muppim had endured his disappointments and his loneliness with great calmness, but the expression of such interest and sympathy overcame him. The tall boy who had begun to attract attention at the tavern where he stayed, was actually in tears. Tears of grateful joy were not the only evidence that Muppim gave of the state of his heart. No! his prayers that night were full of loving trust in his Saviour, and deep thankfulness for all his mercies.

XXI.

A Resolution.

THOUGH Muppim had received a flat refusal at Delmont & Child's when he had applied to be admitted there as a clerk, he found Mr. Thayer's note of introduction put the affair on quite a different footing.

The heads of the establishment, to whom he had been denied admittance, he was now permitted to see, though not without suspicious glances on the part of the clerks. A short interview in the small *sanctum* boarded in at one end of the large establishment, placed Muppim in quite a different light before the persons employed there.

He was no longer a straggling Jew

applying for the situation he did not deserve. He was a person introduced by the well-known John Thayer, and promptly provided with occupation in the lace department of the great "store," where he soon showed himself quite at home. It was a new thing to Muppim to be tied down to regular hours, and to be kept on his feet through the long day.

Naomi had accommodated herself to his tastes, and many a time Muppim had been reading in his own room, while his mother was waiting upon customers. Now there was no mother to come in between Muppim and his round of duties. Here was a new opportunity for the exercise of Christian patience and cheerfulness. Muppim must lay aside his studies. He had only time to read a few chapters in his Bible every day. He could no longer pore over it for hours, tracing Christ in Joseph betrayed of his brethren, Moses leading the chosen people, Aaron entering into the holy of holies, or David the God-appointed King of the Jews.

Now was Muppim's time for fulfilling the command to "labor with his own hands," and " in whatsover state he was, therewith to be content."

The selling of laces was not in itself an ennobling occupation, but he could make it so by entering into it as a duty given him by God. His faithfulness, promptness and industry would win the approval of his Saviour, and so each day he would be making his earthly calling a stepping-stone towards heaven. He would serve God in his labor, if he could no longer spend hours in the study of his precious Word.

It seemed very strange to Muppim to be at his ordinary occupations on the last day of the week,—the Jewish Sabbath. He found it hard to cast off the idea that he was doing wrong, as he stood behind the counter, when he had been wont to be in the synagogue.

Saturday became to him a day of preparation for the true Christian Sabbath. As the old feelings and old associations came up, he recalled the words of the Son of man, who had spoken of himself as "Lord of the Sabbath." He dwelt on the glory of that day when Jesus rose from the tomb, and the first day of the week became the best of days to all Christians— the Lord's day.

Very welcome to Muppim was the true rest that was sure for him on Sunday morning. Then he might give his thoughts wholly to the Saviour, and study his precious word, without haste or interruption.

To worship with Christians was a most welcome privilege to Muppim. At church he felt himself among friends, though in the midst of strangers. He was one among Christ's people, when he has specially promised to be in the midst of them.

Muppim was beginning to feel that he ought to be openly acknowledged as a follower of Jesus, and this conviction was suddenly forced upon him as an immediate duty.

He was surprised one Sunday by hearing the clergyman call on the persons to be baptized to come forward. A young man and two elderly women came up with their witnesses, and in the presence of the congregation, were baptized in the name of the Father, Son, and Holy Ghost. Of course the ceremony was deeply interesting to Muppim, but he was even more interested in the sermon that followed. With earnestness the faithful minister urged upon all who would be owned by the Saviour at the last day, to acknowledge him now, in the ways in which he has appointed. He has commanded that those who believe shall be baptized. He has given to his true people the privilege of taking the Lord's Supper in remembrance of him. They cannot well be Christians who refuse to be baptized in his name, and will not take the bread and wine at his holy table.

As Muppim listened, his resolution was taken. A minister of Christ certainly would not turn away from a stranger, who sought to be baptized in the name of his Master. When the worshippers had scattered away from the church, a tall young Jew still stood waiting without.

What Christian minister does not feel his heart warm towards a Jew seeking to draw near to the true King of Israel? Who does not deem it a privilege to guide one of the ancient people of God into the kingdom of heaven? With such a request as Muppim had to propose, he was sure to be met with open arms. Six weeks he had been a lonely stranger, and now at once he had found a real friend. For six weeks he had seen no one with whom he could speak on the subject nearest his heart, but now the aged minister rejoiced with him, that he had been led to know the Crucified as the Messiah.

That Sunday noon, Muppim went not to his humble boarding-place. At the minister's own table he sat down with a Christian family, and was rejoiced over with great joy.

Little children looked at him with loving interest, as a real Jew, as were Paul and Peter, and Moses and Elijah. A motherly Christian heart expressed its warm sympathy for a son of Israel brought home to his Father's house.

The day for Muppim's baptism was fixed. The aged minister saw no reason for delay in the case of one who so "believed with all his heart."

"Your name is a peculiar one, my young friend; you have now an opportunity to change it if you will," said the clergyman, in concluding their conversation.

"I hope to have a 'new name' in the New Jerusalem," said Muppim, slightly coloring. "Here, I would rather keep the Hebrew name my parents gave me. I am not ashamed of being a Jew! My mother knows me by that name, and it binds me, too, to my dear twin-brother. If we could only be baptized together, as we once together received our names as Jews!"

Ah! how Muppim's heart yearned for his absent brother at that moment.

"We will pray for that brother; he may yet be led into the truth!" said the clergyman.

With the earnestness of those who really want that for which they pray, Muppim joined in the petitions then offered for his absent brother and for the whole house of Israel.

Would that the air were full of prayers for the peculiar people,—then would they begin to seek the Messiah, and learn to know " him of whom Moses and the prophets did write."

XXII.

A Surprise.

A FEW days after his interview with the old clergyman, Muppim was one morning going, at his usual early hour, to his place of business.

Suddenly a large dog jumped upon him, and he was nearly knocked down by the joyous signs of recognition given by the excited animal.

"Why, Bravo!" cried Muppim, in astonishment.

This repetition of his name sent Bravo off in another series of gambols, which said, almost as plainly as spoken language, how glad he was to see his Jewish friend. Bravo seemed to have more to say than a mere "How d'ye do?" for he began to pull at Muppim in a decided manner, intimating that he would be followed, whether Muppim chose it or no.

To a hotel near at hand he led the way, and did not stop until the willing Muppim stood at a bed-room door, at which Bravo scratched most vigorously.

"You've found him, I know," said Charlie Fay, giving admittance to his friend and the dog.

Muppim had only time to promise a long interview in the evening, and then he forced himself to his usual punctual appearance at the store.

If Muppim made wrong change two or three times that day, and put up the Valenciennes laces in the Brussels-point box, he must be excused; his mind was in such a state of excitement and confusion that it was hard for him to attend to his ordinary occupations.

His persevering attempt to be faithful in his duties during the day, were more than rewarded by his long, long interview with Charlie in the evening.

Charlie had actually seen Huppim, and had a good talk with him. Frequent as Charlie's letters had been, they had never been able to tell more than that Jacob's family were well, but refusing to have any intercourse with the blind boy who had had so large a share in Muppim's change of faith.

Charlie's news for Muppim were not all good news; he had to describe a fire by night, when the whole block of buildings in which he lived had been burnt, the inmates only escaping with their lives. He had to own that Jacob Myers' shop on the corner caught like tinder, and was consumed long before the brick buildings next which it stood. He gratefully described the joy of Naomi when she was sure that all her family were safe, and Jacob's wondering confusion, when he knew that he had lost all his property, had disturbed his mind; he could not take hold of the idea that his hard earnings were consumed in a night. The expensive laces that had taken the place of the cheap edgings of old were now but ashes. Jacob was a poor man once more. It was in vain that Huppim spoke of himself as almost grown and able to take care of the family. Jacob cried like a child, and would not be comforted, though Ard wiped his father's eyes with a vigor that ought to have done some good.

All this and more Charlie had heard from Huppim, who in the general confusion had not forgotten his blind friend, and had made sure of his safety. Since that terrible night Charlie and Huppim had had a long talk, and never meant to be wholly separated again.

Naomi in her softened state had given Huppim permission to count Charlie once more among his friends, and poor Jacob cared for little now but the loss of his dear money.

Muppim felt it a sore trial to be cut off from his family in the time of their affliction; he longed to comfort his mother, and to consult with Huppim as to what was to be done to better their fallen fortunes.

On one thing Muppim promptly resolved: he had his first month's payment yet untouched—he would forward it to Huppim through Mrs. Fay, and say how gladly he would devote all that he could earn to the use of his father and the rest of the family.

When this resolution was taken, Muppim felt a little relieved, and then he said, "Forgive me, Charlie; in my interest about our people, I had almost forgotten you. Did you lose anything at the fire? Now I want to know what brought you here, and who is with you; you said you would tell me all about it to-night."

"And so I will; we lost everything! The house was all my mother owned in the world. The letting of some of the rooms, you know, gave us our little income. Oh, Muppim! I never felt what it was to be really blind, until I knew that my mother needed some one to earn for her her daily bread. She is too delicate, you know, and I know, to support herself and me. Oh, Muppim, that was my bitter hour! when we could feel on our faces the heat of the burning house, opposite to which we stood, and I knew that we were left destitute. Huppim, he was at my side, full of hope, saying that now was the time for the boys of the family to come forward and show what was in them! I showed what was in me then! I blush to think of it—I actually cried, Muppim, I so longed to be my mother's protector! Then there came a sweet whisper to my mind that I could call on the great Heavenly Friend, who has made such promises to the widow and the fatherless. I gave myself up to him; I asked him to provide for us in his own way, and to keep down my proud heart, that longed to do the work God had not laid out for me. As I stood there by my mother, I heard Mr. Thayer's voice in my ear;—he took us to his house, and he has been, oh, so kind!"

"He has taken charge of you—I know it—just like him!" said Muppim, warmly.

"Better than that! better than that, Muppim! he is going to help me to maintain myself," Charlie quickly replied. "He had seen an advertisement for an organist in this city, and so he would start right off with me, to let the people hear me play, and see what can be done. He has been out all day about it, and to-morrow I am to try in the church."

"I know you will succeed; you are sure of a blessing," exclaimed Muppim, affectionately.

"That would be a blessing, indeed," said Charlie; "but now I must send you off, for it is getting late. I shall be too nervous to-morrow to do well, if I don't have my sleep."

"I shall write the letter to your mother to-night,—and you are sure she will hand the money to Huppim, and tell him all my message?" said Muppim.

"Sure of it! I shouldn't wonder if you should hear from Huppim himself shortly. He did not know where you were, until I told him, just before we came away. Muppim, he loves you as he does his own eyes."

"I believe it! I believe it!" responded Muppim; then, with a hearty "Good-night," he parted from his friend.

XXIII.

The Outward Sign.

MUPPIM had expected to come up to his baptism without a friend as his witness, but the case was far different. When the young Jew stood up before the congregation to be baptized in the name of the Father, Son, and Holy Ghost, it was with Mr. Thayer and Charlie Fay at his side.

They who had striven to lead him to Jesus, were with him when he openly avowed his Lord and Master, and was received into his visible church. The services of the day were most appropriate. While the Crucifixion was particularly commemorated, the Jews seemed to be constantly remembered.

Muppim's heart swelled, and his whole

soul prayed, as he joined in the petitions, "O merciful God, who hast made all men, and hatest nothing that thou hast made, nor desirest the death of a sinner, but rather that he should be converted and live; have mercy upon all Jews, Turks, infidels, and heretics; and take from them all ignorance, hardness of heart, and contempt of thy word; and so fetch them home, blessed Lord, to thy flock, that they may be saved among the remnant of the true Israelites, and be made one fold under one shepherd, Jesus Christ our Lord, who liveth and reigneth, with thee and the Holy Spirit, one God, world without end. Amen."

When the text was announced, Muppim's attention was in a moment fixed. "And so all Israel shall be saved: as it is written, there shall come out of Zion a Deliverer, and shall turn away ungodliness from Jacob." Rom. xi. 26.

Very earnestly did the minister speak to his hearers of the peculiar people of God, to whom such precious promises were made. He called on all Christians to labor for the conversion of the Jews, and and to do it in faith, knowing that the time will surely come when Israel shall again be exalted, and Christ be the King of the Jews.

Very precious words were these to Muppim. New faith and new hope for his own dear family sprung up in his heart, and he rejoiced over them, as if he already saw them bowing the knee to Jesus, and hailing him as Lord.

XXIV.

The True Passover.

WHEN Muppim entered church on the Sunday after the Friday on which he was baptized, it was with peculiar solemnity. He was that day for the first time to take the bread and wine of the communion, in memory of the body and blood of Christ given for us on the Cross.

This was the Passover season with the Jews, and Muppim's thoughts had been much with his own people. Now he was to understand how " old things have passed away, and all things have become new."

In his ears were sounded the solemn words, " Christ our Passover is sacrificed for us, therefore let us keep the feast.

" Not with the old leaven, neither with

the leaven of malice and wickedness; but with the unleavened bread of sincerity and truth."

Now, for the first time, the young Jew understood the whole beauty of the sacred feast of the Christians, wherein Christ, who is the Lamb slain for us, is remembered, even as the Lamb of the Passover had for hundreds of years pointed out his coming. As the blood on the door-posts of Israel preserved their houses from the angel of death, so Muppim felt his Saviour's blood would make sure his salvation.

Gladly would Muppim have welcomed his own dear ones to gather with him round the table of the Lord to keep the true Passover, but that privilege was still denied him. Yet, he did not lack even human sympathy in that solemn hour. His hand was in that of his blind friend, whom he gently guided to the place where they were appointed to kneel. There were many in the congregation to rejoice over the converted Jew, and welcome him to the Christian church.

With Christ's family Muppim kept that day the Passover, and the blessing of Christ was upon him, even that "peace which passeth all understanding."

XXV.

A Removal.

THE fire that had broken up Jacob Myers' home had done away with the restriction by which it was forbidden to mention the absent Muppim.

Jacob Myers was no longer the head of his family. The poor Jew, who had set his heart upon his earthly gains, could not withstand the shock which deprived him of what he loved best. He seemed as one in a dream, or as a lost child wandering in a strange country. There was no wildness in his manner. He was gentle, touchingly gentle, but clung to Naomi as to his stay and guide.

Huppim plainly saw that they could not long retain even the humble lodgings they had taken. There was not enough left of

Jacob's earnings to keep his family from actual want. His heart yearned for his absent brother. The two he thought might now sustain the family burden, " shoulder to shoulder." Though young, they might beat back the storm of adversity.

Naomi, too, thought much of Muppim. She fancied their present trial was a judgment upon them for their harshness to their patient, dutiful son. She longed to see that son, and ask his forgiveness for the past.

Most welcome then were direct tidings from Muppim. Huppim's joyousness seemed to come back to him, as he looked upon the letter to Mrs. Fay which his brother's hand had so lately traced.

Naomi was completely melted when she received the earnings of her banished son,—so promptly sent to her in her hour of need and trouble. This, surely, was a forgiveness of which the Jew knows nothing. This was of the same spirit as Muppim's gentleness under rebuke.

Month after month a portion of Muppim's earnings was forwarded to his father's family. Huppim chafed sorely at his own inaction, and when Muppim at length wrote to him that there was a situation vacant in the establishment where he had won favor, and he had liberty to offer it to him, Huppim at once saw the wisdom of accepting it.

"I cannot be left alone with your father; we will all go to Muppim. I know he will not meet us harshly," said Naomi, in a low, humble tone.

Ard gave a bound of joy at the good tidings, and ran to communicate the news to his father. His prattling tongue easily told what Naomi dreaded to mention.

"Muppim—yes, to Muppim. He will know what we had better do," said Jacob, helplessly. So the matter was settled.

XXVI.

A Christian Family.

AS Muppim and Huppim and Charlie Fay had shared their childish pleasures, they now shared their present interests and cares.

Charlie was the organist in a large church, and occupied in practising and perfecting himself in his art; he felt it a solemn privilege to have a share in the praise of the great congregation. With the tones of the solemn organ there went up notes more welcome to the angels—even the grateful homage of the blind boy's heart, uplifted to his Lord. Charlie's occupation was such as kept ever in his mind the great object of existence, and he was most useful to his young friends in reminding them that the cares of this life may check the good seed, as well as its pomps and its pleasures.

The daily meeting with his blind friend was a constant help to Muppim in his effort to serve God without worldliness, and, in the midst of business, to be "fervent in spirit.'

Not a word passed between Naomi and Muppim on the subject of their separation, when they once more met. The mother's loving embrace told her joy at the reunion, and Muppim had already acted out his free forgiveness for the past.

Ard's delight knew no bounds; he constantly gave his approving testimony to his brother's consistent life, by declaring "nobody was as good as brother Muppim."

It was touching to see Muppim's tender care of his broken-spirited father; he was never impatient of the poor man's childish questionings and weak babble. For him the best seat was placed ; to him Muppim rendered honor, and for him daily prayed.

Such dutiful conduct, such entire forgiveness acted day by day upon Naomi ; she could not withstand the evidence of the truth of a religion which thus spoke in a language which could not be mistaken.

The happy time came at last, when the Jewish Passover was no more kept at Jacob Myers' ; as a Christian family, the mother and her sons knelt at the Christian communion ; Ard was being trained up in the Christian faith.

The sorrowful days of his first embracing the truth seemed to Muppim as a sad dream of the past, to be forgotten in the grateful joy of the present.

Poor Jacob was yet in the house, a memento of their Jewish days ; but even he was catching the Christian hymns from Ard, and, as it were, groping in his darkness after Jesus, the crucified.

XXVII.

Conclusion.

YEARS passed on. Huppim's talent for business could not escape the notice of his experienced employers; he was gradually promoted to positions of trust, until at length he was only next to the heads of the firm in his influence in the concern.

Now he had a handsome salary, and a fair promise of being one day a partner in the establishment, where his value was thus acknowledged.

Muppim saw with pleasure his brother's success in the career for which he was so well fitted. For his own part, he had maintained the respect of his employers, but the talent for money-making was not one of his peculiar gifts—his heart was elsewhere, in another work, and that his brother well knew.

"Muppim," said Huppim, affectionately, one evening, "Muppim, I want to do something for our own people; I cannot rest until more effort is made to lead them to the knowledge of Jesus."

Muppim grasped his brother's hand, and said, "That subject is on my mind day and night!"

"I have a plan by which we can both do something for this object," said Huppim.

Muppim listened with earnestness.

"This is it: I am prospered; the care of the family will not hang heavily upon me now. I want you to devote yourself to study; you are meant for better things than buying and selling. I want you to preach the gospel to our own people. We will have a common purse; I will be the merchant and you shall be the minister, so we can both work for God in our own way."

Muppim was completely overcome, as much by his brother's delicate generosity, as by the fulfilment of his own dearest hopes. This was the opportunity for which he had so longed, during his years of patient industry in a calling most uncongenial to his tastes.

For a few moments Muppim was unable to speak; then he said, " Huppim, I accept the offer as freely as it is made, and may God make me a faithful teacher of the truth to his ancient people."

So the twin-brothers joined their hands to make known the religion of Jesus to the children of Israel. So should all Christians join their prayers, their means, and their efforts for this great object.

The veil is more over the *hearts* than the *heads* of the Jews. They will not, they do not " search the Scriptures." They need to be urged to read the Old Testament, which they acknowledge, and so they will be ready to embrace the New.

The Lord Jesus himself said, "If they believe not Moses and the prophets, neither will they believe though one rose from the dead." The Jews must learn to study the Old Testament, praying that they may be guided to the true Messiah.

When Israel will seek to know the Lord, then shall the God of Jacob pour out his blessing upon them, and turn them unto him, as with one mind and one heart.

We cannot follow Muppim in his career of usefulness, or tell how Naomi rejoiced to see her prayers at the birth of her twins fulfilled in God's own way.

We may not linger to describe Ard's joy over every Jew converted to the truth, or Charlie Fay's gratitude at the success of the ministry of his friend, for whom he so constantly prayed.

The faithful laborer has a sure promise of blessing on his labors, but not in this world is counted up the increase.

When the Passovers and Communions of earth are over, then, at the marriage supper of the Lamb, it shall be seen who have sought out the "lost sheep of the house of Israel," and guided them to that blessed region, where there shall be "one fold and one shepherd." In the New Jerusalem, they "who have turned many to righteousness shall shine as the stars forever and ever;" and they who have labored for the Jews upon earth, will certainly be abundantly rewarded by the King of the Jews, the everlasting Son of the Father

THE END.

www.ingramcontent.com/pod-product-compliance
Lightning Source LLC
Chambersburg PA
CBHW020901230426
43666CB00008B/1264